Violin Making

by Walter H. Mayson

CONTENTS.

PAGE INTRODUCTION . . . .

CHAPTER I.

SELECTION OF WOOD . . . .

CHAPTER II.

THE BACK . . . .

CHAPTER III.

PURFLING . . . .

CHAPTER IV.

BENDING THE PURFLING . . . .

CHAPTER V.

MODELLING THE BACK . . . .

CHAPTER VI.

WORKING OUT THE BACK . . . .

CHAPTER VII.

THE BELLY . . . .

CHAPTER VIII.

THICKNESSES OF THE BELLY . . . .

CHAPTER IX.

THE SOUNDHOLES . . . .

CHAPTER X.

THE BASS BAR . . . .

CHAPTER XI.

THE RIBS . . . .

CHAPTER XII.

FIXING RIBS, ETC. . . . .

CHAPTER XIII.

FIXING THE BELLY . . . .

CHAPTER XIV.

THE SCROLL . . . .

CHAPTER XV.

FIXING NECK, FINGERBOARD, ETC. . . . .

CHAPTER XVI.

OF VARNISH AND VARNISHING . . . . . .

CHAPTER XVII.

FITTING UP FOR USE . . . .

CHAPTER XVIII.

CONCLUSION . . . .

PREFACE.

I do not like Prefaces.

They remind me somewhat of awaiting dinner in a drawing-room after a long walk in wintry weather. It is one thing to get there an occasional whiff of viands cooking in the basement of the house, and quite another to feel the same accentuate your gnawings of hunger.

Therefore, did I touch on motives for writing this book, or sketch outlines of heads of matters to follow in detail, I should engage little or no attention, so shall simply refer you who may read this preface, which is only a fraud, to the matter embodied in the following pages, for which, at least, I claim Honesty.

WALTER H. MAYSON.

62, OXFORD STREET, C.-ON-M., MANCHESTER.

The great success of the previous edition, and the numerous letters sent in praise of "VIOLIN MAKING," prompts me (the author's son) to take the opportunity of saying a few words, and to thank the public for their appreciation of the work.

I have received many communications (several from abroad) from enthusiasts, bestowing the warmest praise on the writer as a Maker and an Author; and all are unanimous in declaring that the simple and explicit style of the work has enabled them to readily grasp the difficulties pertaining to the Violin as a work of Art. These correspondents (who are quite strangers to me) have also greatly commended the high class appearance of the volume, particularly the excellence of the fine illustrations. Such expressions of approval would have been gratifying to the late W. H. MAYSON, who, as the maker of over 800 instruments, had attained complete mastery over his work. Therefore the reader can have every confidence in faithfully following all his methods and strictly adhering to every detail set forth in this volume.

STANSFIELD MAYSON.

48, OXFORD ROAD, MANCHESTER, June, 1909.

INTRODUCTION.

Many admirable works on this interesting subject have appeared in several languages, but, to my mind, in a form too sternly technical, cold, if I may be allowed--the writers barely in touch with the anxious youth or man, who, as amateur, yearns to get at that knowledge of correct construction without which he scarce may hope to become a professional violin maker, some notable instances to the contrary, all the same.

I hold simplicity to be the very essence of the conveyance of matter from mind to mind, as in words; from mind to eye, as by pencil, brush, or chisel; palpable or otherwise, the impression intended should be beyond doubt, and that this end may be secured, mystification by high flown figures of rhetoric, or false drawing, or sculpture out of line or proportion, must at the outset of all work, art work above all, be sternly trodden under foot, and the solid and truthful experience of ripe years offered with the same eagerness to impart information as it is awaited by the student.

If you spend ten minutes in telling a man what form an oval assumes, when you can, by drawing it for him on a blackboard, present it before his eye in one minute, and more to the purpose, you not only waste your own time but his also, and commit a breach of trust, in that you mislead and mystify when it was your duty to faithfully guide and teach in all sincerity and simplicity.

Therefore I propose, in the following pages, to adopt an entirely different treatment from any work I have had the honour of studying on the construction of the violin; writing as though orally addressing the students, or those anxious to become students, of the whole world--a vast semicircle of bright faced, intelligent creatures before me, following eagerly every movement of the numerous tools I use in the extremely delicate manipulations of the instrument as it almost imperceptibly assumes that form so noble and so beloved, and almost devouring the, I hope, lucid explanations, which, from time to time, I may think it necessary to make, and which will appear as letterpress, the illustrations speaking for themselves as the work progresses.

This little thing that I am about to make, this shell of scarce sixteen ounces in weight, constructed of about eighty pieces of wood, and united by glue as one complete whole; this, that is a mighty factor, where mirth, and mirth only, is to the fore, in its embodiment; this, that draws from the soul the tear which has long yearned for an outlet of intense sympathy such as it now finds; this, that beautifies as it ennobles to the pinnacle of sublimity all music, even as it takes it by the hand, guides and cements it.

What is the origin of this violin or fiddle, and to what country does the honour belong?

To this day its origin, as a violin, is a contested point, and in my opinion will so remain; that is to say, how it worked its way, so to speak, out of now obsolete instruments, into what it is (for it was certainly a growth, not a complete conception), by whom it was so worked, and where--these points, aggravating points, if you will, seeing there is nothing of clearness around them, had better be left by you where they are; for, when Germany and Italy are supposed strong claimants, and assert a right not borne out by fact, according as I read the so-called evidence, it were futile to enter into discussion destined to have no satisfactory result.

But, though we cannot give this thing a "local habitation," we can give it a name, aye, and a name destined to live as long as lips move to pronounce it.

And we can make it noble, too, of exquisite shape and colour, possessing a voice capable of we know not what compass and expression; just as we can turn it out by the thousand, degrading the name of art to which it has the impudence to lay claim, on every feature of its brazen face stamped that nationality which, so far from seeking, it in vain tries to get rid of.

If in the progress of these lectures I touch on cause and effect in relation to acoustics, my remarks will be merely superficial, sufficient for my purpose, but not for him who wishes fully to master this absorbing doctrine, which he will find most useful should his purpose be to try experiments in relation to tone.

As to giving diagrams of supposed eccentric or concentrated curves relative to the vibration of the back or belly of the violin, or to the motions of the air waves, rapid or slow, that I do not intend to do; others have done that, with what benefit to their work or their supposed pupils we may probably ascertain later should more be added on the subject.

Therefore, gentlemen, if it be your strong, stern desire to sit out these somewhat prolonged lectures, whilst I endeavour to make for you, step by step, a true work of art, according to my conception and in strict accordance with my deeply thought-out principles, and with such tools as I find most simple and most suitable for the work I have to do, then do so, and I shall feel highly honoured and very proud; but, if a lighter, more trivial creation will, or would satisfy your (craving I will not call it, that suggests pertinacity, a great end being in view), say, passing fancy, then I would rather see vacant the place occupied by you, as in such an one I should take no interest whilst speaking or working, just as that one would appear of too shallow a nature to absorb lasting benefit from what was said or done by me.

In concluding this introduction to a subject which I hold to be of much moment as the leading instrument, never to be replaced by another, let me beg of you to abandon a half-hearted consideration of its adoption in actual work later on, unless you be prepared to suffer for this fine art, a member of the body of which it is your present thought to become; for, be assured, there will be suffering, which will dog your progress; aye, and the greater your talent, so much more will be jealousy of it, from those, at least, so on the alert to decry that which they cannot create; so much more will be contumely; so much more will be innuendoes which can not be met openly, as they certainly will not be in the slimy words and manner of utterance of bitter heartlessness, that is to say, if you be made of that stuff which presents to the world an artist, who is nothing if he be not noble.

Contumely, jealousy, suffering, but not necessarily failure therefrom, despite an occasional reverse, hard to bear; nay, the feeling that there is something good in you, and worthy of acknowledgment and acceptance by the world later on, will spur you to greater exertion, and act as a mantle beneath which you may shelter from the cold shower hurled by those so prone to drown or starve that which, not feeling themselves, they are determined shall neither spring from nor be passed to the credit of others-- enthusiasm.

VIOLIN MAKING

CHAPTER I.

SELECTION OF WOOD.

Many persons of good, practical ability, and moderately versed in the laws of acoustics, with an eye for form, and not deficient in a certain conception of art as art; who have the instinct to check any approach to vulgarity, and work on lines, curves and thicknesses, more or less true, elegant, and the best for producing fine tone, have seen, and will yet again see, their efforts of small avail, cast aside, never to assume even mediocre rank in the stern array of violins of modern make, much less of those of ancient Italy, merely because the wood chosen for the instrument made is of an inferior, probably worthless character, which would have been employed to much more purpose had it been used in the construction of a windmill, or the shaft of a mine.

That is to say, if, as I presume and premise, the first germ in the conception of construction of the instrument be tone, as most assuredly tone it ought to be, not to the detriment of appearance, or to its subjugation as an art work, but as an adjunct or accessory of such importance that it is apparent it must imperatively assume pre-eminence; just as we forget the plain box of the 甫 lian harp the moment the strings are struck by the passing gale into the most exquisite chords; as, on the contrary, do we seem to wish for no song from the tropical bird of magnificent plumage, and express no surprise that none comes from it. I may put this more plainly as I proceed, and in more homely words. What I want to lay before you now, and must insist upon, is, that you seek for tone, tone before all. Tone you must get at all cost; and to get it, you must have as choice wood as ever can be procured, and fashion it into a singing shell, so that from it pure music may be evolved.

Then you must get this choice wood, but how? Now, the word "choice" presupposes variety from which to select, as I select or choose so-and-so, which is my choice. But I use the word in another way, on the face of it bearing the same significance, but not quite so. I say it is fine, of superb quality for my purpose, which is the emission of the grandest tone possible, rapid, strong and sonorous, from two plates of wood, becoming, if they possess these attributes, choice to me.

We will consider the back wood first. I have thirty pieces from which to take one, which shall act in conjunction with the belly, to be selected later on. Some are plain, pear tree, in fact; others are also plain (I mean as regards figure, or flames, as the Germans say), and of sycamore, others are of maple. I do not select a handsome one for its beauty, just as surely as I do not reject an ordinary one for its plainness. This will show you at once that I am seeking for that which, to my mind, will yield me the finest tone.

Well, but we must determine this before we go farther, and in the rough, the initial stage of the wood, supposed to be old, and fit for the under table of the instrument about to be made. I will try this one of maple--moderately handsome, looking old, but, I fear, not quite honest, as it is too heavy for its bulk. I take the half of it (it being in two parts) and about one third from the top, having the thick edge, or that to which, later on, I join the other thick edge, close to my left ear, my left first finger and thumb grasping it there so as just to free the body for vibration, I strike it near the lower part of the thin side rapidly, with the large joint of the first finger of my right hand. With what result? That of strengthening, almost confirming, my suspicion of its honesty. For I find a lack of energy, of resonance, and of that quality to which I apply the word sympathy. It is crude, it is dull, and it will not do for my purpose.

Well, but as so many go by what so many advocate and so many do, why not try it by placing the plate in this vice, and applying a well rosined bow to draw forth its sonority, etc., etc.? I will do so. I fear many of you, even just in front of me, will scarce gather much from the thin, miserable stuff which the wood says is its voice, and which its vendors assert to be old, well dried, and that for which it was bought. And I pity, indeed, those receding into the misty background, for nought of this squeak will they hear, and well for them! But as this second test is condemnatory and more and more convinces me of the unworthiness of the wood for a violin of high class (or of any violin destined to live), let me put it to a still more searching one, in fact, to two, neither of which, I venture to assert, will it bear.

I clamp it to the bench and proceed to cut with a gouge several pieces from the surface of an area of about three inches, close to the thick edge. These I lay aside as No. 1. Deeper, but still from the same area, more, as No. 2. Deeper, but not now as deep as before, for an obvious reason, according to my theory, which is my last heap and No. 3. Now, gentlemen, will you pass round this handful. No. 1, what is there about it? Really, an acid smell! and No. 2, the same, but less pungent; No. 3, less still! Well, there you have absolute proof of roguery, which, if it were lacking in strength, would be borne out by the diminution of the lying brown colour towards the centre of the wood, that colour, not of age, but of fraud, which, named acid, affects the surface more than the interior, and which the novice gloats over as old and pure as God's mountains!

Well, but in addition to these two farther tests of smell and colour--making wood, almost green wood, of probably not more than four years old, appear to the ignorant one hundred--there is another which I often use, and that is, as I do now, I make the plate rigid, but free to vibrate, so as to allow those mysterious motions play, and I place my ear at one extremity whilst I scratch or scrape, or move the rosined bow over the other.

With a similar result--the tone is not what I want, nor what it ought to be from a piece of really old, well grown wood. But mind, it does not follow that, given these conditions, the genuine thing would be what I want; but there would be more likelihood of its being so, and less annoyance in laying it aside us worthless, as I do this, selecting, for a second trial, a piece of what I call crabbed wood, known by a peculiar curl, and its very handsome and uncommon appearance.

But before I test this, I must tell you that none but a workman of great skill would undertake to put it to use, as it is so "crabbed," so twisted in its fibre, that on the least carelessness of the artist, out flies a chip from where it should not, and a very delicate operation is resorted to in consequence to amend the blunder--insertion of a slip which must match the grain of the original every way, not only in flame, but even just as the flash of that fire falls in its movement when it becomes part of a violin.

I have said earlier "I do not select handsome wood for its beauty," etc., and the loveliness of this piece must not tempt me to sacrifice what I hold of more consequence--tone. But I should do so did I now choose it; for it is weak where it should be strong, and poor, flabby and wretched from the view of acoustics.

So you see how difficult it is even for the eye of experience and the mind of knowledge to wade through the vile to the pure uncontaminated: how much more so him, the sanguine amateur, at once the plaything and the dupe of those who do not scruple to beguile him by the one to the safe usage of the other!

Still, do not let it be supposed that this slight tinge of the minor key is intended to make you despond; on the contrary, I want to show you better things, and mean to do so. And should the doing of it seem to prolong this part of my address beyond moderate limits, my excuse must be its deep importance.

I have laid aside three pieces of sycamore, all, as I believe, very good for the back I purpose making. One is what is called "on the quarter," the other two "on the slab" (these terms I shall explain later, when I have fully spoken of the selection of wood). The two on the slab are in one piece, of course; the one on the quarter in two pieces, one of which, while I have been speaking, I have glued slightly, but firmly, to an upright support of glass, made very rough at the place where I fix the plate, so that the glue may the better hold, temporarily.

The glass, being a non-conductor (or, if it respond in any way, however infinitesimally, it does not perceptibly affect my plate, and in no way my argument), leaves me the absolute control of this wood, and I proceed to lay an English lever watch on several places of it, keeping my ear near to that nodal point where I know will come the inner bout, or D of the violin, consequently the bridge, which I mark with a X. The tick-tack of the watch varies in strength as I get farther from or nearer to a nodal point, as, of course, it was bound to do; but, from experience, it is a fine-toned piece of wood. I detach it from the glass rod, and I try it by my finger and thumb test, and the vibrations and their quality are all I could desire. The signs of age appear genuine: the small pieces I cut from it do not give out any smell which they should not, and I pronounce the wood honest. I try the two whole backs, on the slab: both are good, one very fine in tone and handsome in appearance, which I finally select for the violin about to be made.

Well, but you may say, in all your experiments, it appears to us the result is a question of degree. Exactly, a question of degree, as purity of air is, but who chooses the foul when he can live in the pure? As with flowers in their unassuming simplicity up to such elegance of form, colour and fragrance, that we stand amazed before them! As with man, from the worse than bestial state to which intemperance and crime have brought him, to the calm majesty of that eminence, attained only by the love of truth, of self-government, and scorn of evil-doing!

This question of degree strikes at the root of the whole subject before you: for, upon how you answer it, or to what person or persons you repair for guidance in the selection of wood (being novices), will depend in a great measure your success or failure in the instrument yet unmade.

The upper table or belly, made of pine, Swiss pine by preference, is the most important factor in the production of tone, consequently that to which the chief attention of the artist should be directed. No matter how good be his back or his ribs, or the sweep of his lines or curves, or quality of his varnish and its elasticity or its superb colour, the selection of wood for his upper table or belly, or soundboard, must be his chief concern, and neither money nor energy spared to secure the best.

Well, I have by me several, of various degrees of excellence, and some of very doubtful reputation; nay, I may at once say they are bad--even by their look they are bad. This one is fairly straight in the grain, but it has been dried artificially, not as were the backs, yet more wickedly treated--impregnated with a deleterious something having the power of destroying a germ destined, if left to age, to become the soul of resonance, bringing it at once to a wretched maturity, its cells starved so, that when the strain of three hours' play in a hot room is put upon it, dumb is its voice, poor at the best, and it is played out.

Do you not see that the soft part of the wood running between the lines or reeds, and where lie the cells of the pine, are too rapidly agitated, and cannot possibly hold their own under such worn-out conditions? whereas, given honest wood and genuine age, we should get strength to resist, and from such resistance would come what we seek, richness, possible only from sound resonance.

For these cells must have the vigour of mature age, if that age be 150 years when naturally dried, in them; and my contention is, that the soundest is that which has not been robbed of its sap, as turpentine, before it be felled on the mountain side; but cut when well-grown, and well looked after for some years, then cut on the quarter (of which, later), and left for at least seven more years before we use it; and mind, even then, it is new wood.

I say, this is my contention, and how I account for many superior, great-souled violins, which it has been my hard struggle to produce, yet now gaze on with pride; almost glorying in that enthusiasm which enabled me to combat all against my theory, and do that which I believe was done two hundred years ago, to such fine issues, reviled or not for so doing, is now to me of little consequence.

Yet you must be told that there has been fierce, very fierce, controversy on this point, some going half-way and asserting only a portion of the sap should be withdrawn; some (and one of them a great chemist, a friend of mine) fighting hard to have it all taken away, and artificially dried after that! Does nature do this to the lungs of a Madame Patti or a Sims Reeves before she turns them on the world? Nonsense!

But it is tests you want, and I will supply another, somewhat original. This piece I called above, bad, I lay aside, as No. 1; another, worse in grain, but, I believe, honest, as far as having the sap left in it goes, but not old, No. 2; and a magnificent piece of very old Swiss pine, brown, and honestly brown, with, probably, two or three hundred years of exposure as a beam in a Swiss chalet (for from that place and that dwelling I am prepared to prove it comes to me), which I number 3.

The No. 1 is what I call feverish in its vibrations, and would be certain to give any instrument a hollow tone, an instrument cuddled, tempered, and made to fit the ear of the expected purchaser by the experienced one who has it to dispose of. The tone would not be intermittent--if it were that, we might have some hope of ultimate fulness and fair quality; but it would be loud and coarse; bawling when it should be energetic, yet somewhat hoarse, scarce knowing where to vibrate, it being capable of doing so, and well, when fairly mature. But that which, like the brazen actress, has a word or a sentence ready at any moment, and in any key and in any pitch, say good-bye to that at once.

The No. 2 will be good in about four or five years, but would be bad to work just now, so we will take up No. 3, upon which I must dwell somewhat.

I can depend on the gentleman's word who procured this and other pieces for me; and I imagine his estimate of age is much under the approximate date, for I should say it was nearer three than two hundred years old. The colour all through is a mellow brown; the reed is of medium width, well developed, and nearly equal all over, and it is singularly bowed from bottom to top, meeting, when joined (for it is in two parts), just as will a string of a violin when you hold it in both hands, and twang it to test its equal vibration.

Who is bold enough to assert that this is not a piece of finely developed virgin pine, grown on the southern slope of some Alp adjacent to where it had rested so long, in so mean a position for such finely sounding wood which I have proved it to be, yet destined to fill such an honourable place in the grand instrument of which I treat? No one, I venture to reply; but to my mind, and from experience, it is such, the softer part, where run the cells, being firm, full, and mellow to the thumb nail on pressure (showing, I think, good sap lies dried there), which I have found before in such wood, proved to be grand beyond doubt by its superb tone in a violin.

But I must give you, besides my other tests, that to which I occasionally resort. No. 1, you see, is as I intimated, loud and vulgar, ceasing its vibrations the instant I draw away my test of bow, etc., etc., whereas No. 2 does behave better in this respect, but is crude, and must lie some years longer neglected, when it will be interesting again to test it, by me or some other. No. 3 is all I could wish, or was prepared for, so I will hasten to the final trial and bring this lecture to a close, not subjecting this No. 3 to the trial which the others have undergone, as I am quite convinced of its great superiority, but shall, along with the others, put it now to the concluding one.

From each of the three pieces, 1, 2, 3, I cut a slip, and, as you observe, I put No. 1 in this bright clear fire behind me, prepared so that it shall be as nearly free from flame as possible, to enable me to make the manner of burning of each separated piece more real to you.

From what I have said, leading up to what I now do, I imagine you will be somewhat prepared for the manner in which No. 1 burns, and perhaps the other two. But I hardly think you expected such a wretched flare up as you see here, such a fizzing, spluttering, ragged exhibition of imbecility. What of that sonority which could fill a mighty hall where we find five thousand listeners? Is such flabby nonsense as this to be put into an immortal violin, because it purports to be fine Swiss pine at tenpence? But I reverence its ashes, and will lay them aside for a moment, as I wish you to see them alongside the others, when burnt.

No. 2 is all right as to the sap being in it, but it is too volatile, somewhat crackling in its burning, yet far more steady in its flame, not spending its energy in fireworks, nor giving great cracks, like a whip, and a jump afterwards as No. 1, so we will lay aside his ashes.

Now, look at No. 3, as it burns; and do not say, "You invariably have nothing but praise for your best things, how is that?" because, gentlemen, there is no blame which can be laid to them; that is why, and that is all. I ask you to look at this No. 3. It is a steady piece of business altogether. The flame is strong, bright, and well-sustained, with little or no smoke, and it gradually dies down, as, if you will allow my fancy, does he who has grown in uprightness to fine maturity, hale and beautiful to the last. Look at the remains of the three slips. The first is little more than black fluff; I can actually blow it away, poor rubbish! while the second and third are similar to each other, but the No. 3 is more compact, if I may so say, and this is what its excellence before burning would prepare one for.

And do you now wonder that I so insist on every test possible being brought to bear in this important matter of selection? Which of you would hesitate one moment in his choice between these three bellies now? But you must still bear in mind that what I say I bear out by test, others will decry as false, as their theory is as absolutely opposite to mine as the poles. But it will be proved yet, and on stable grounds; and if I, in conjunction with a man of great scientific attainments, succeed, on my theory, in the injection of liquid rosin, or turpentine, into the cells of a piece of broad-grained pine from which we can be sure its original sap has been withdrawn, and keep it well exposed to dry air for seven or so years; by its side a belly, cut from the same piece, in its sapless state; and then make two violins exactly alike in back and thicknesses of plates, etc., of the two pieces of pine, the one raw and sapless, its other half with an injection of rosin; I say we have done somewhat to allay anxiety on such a vital question, and can the more readily meet argument should we triumph on the point of tone--which is our standpoint--or settle down to take the tapped or the untapped indiscriminately.

CHAPTER II.

THE BACK.

I naturally suppose you will supply yourselves with two benches--good, strong, English made, workmanlike things, one of them to be fitted with a single vice, the other with a double one, for joints, and for some work requiring such. And that you will get such tools as will be requisite from time to time for your work.

Then do me the honour of marking very closely how I set about my not too easy employment; for if you follow my ways, you will do well to observe every turn of them; remembering that every part of the building of this little, though mighty, shell is of great importance, and that there is nothing trivial about it.

A prudent and watchful general will be very careful to see his rear is clear of the enemy before he makes an advance after an engagement; so I remember I have to speak to you of wood "on the quarter" and "on the slab" before we go farther.

If you select a large orange, and take it entirely to pieces, you will have by you, without any farther illustration from me, my exact meaning of "on the quarter."

For, when a tree is cut into parts for the violin, it is sawn equally in half, first; then each half into two quarters, and so on, exactly as is the orange subdivided; this is, I hope, clear to you as "on the quarter." I need hardly add that the broad edges, which you join afterwards, making the wood for the upper or lower table look like the roof of a house, are at the outer part of the tree, springing from the centre, where are the broadest rims, as is natural, seeing that youth is there, vigorous and full of sap; whilst the rims decrease to the outer, or bark part, in some cases very decidedly in width, in others more slowly. So you may gather from this why we have the narrow bait, or reed, where the bridge comes, the open reed at the edge. At least, I hope you can see the reason, which is, as generally admitted, and is certainly my view of the matter, the strength is most wanted at the centre of the violin, as at the bridge, which the closeness of the reeds and narrowness of cell passages would supply. The broad reed is more volatile, and we put it to the edges, where it throws off the gathered activity of resonance, recurring so rapidly, which we increase by reducing the thickness of the plate there, bringing about that timbre so rich to the ear of the listener. These remarks apply to the belly, and are offered "on the quarter" only. Wood "on the slab" is never used for the front table in any case, as, cut that way, it would be far too weak.

For "on the slab" means that our orange and our tree are cut through the rings or reeds in flat layers of equal thickness (as required); and it is at once obvious that, in the upper plate, would be not only ugliness of broad, irregular figure of wood, with now and again snatches of the bait as it should be, and as I have endeavoured to show it is; but apart from its general weakness, it would be most irregular as the main vibrator or soundboard, so is entirely discarded.

But both ways of cutting are employed for the back; I have heard tone as fine from one as from the other, yet I think, as a rule, I prefer the quarter to the slab, as being somewhat more resonant and of finer timbre.

At the last moment I have selected the "brother" of my "Elephanta" violin--I mean its back--in one piece, but on the "quarter" in preference to the one on the "slab," so we will now proceed to active work upon it.

I clamp the selected wood to this bench, having the flat side uppermost, and so that I can plane it to a perfect level surface, first at the narrow end, then at the broad, but across the wood, as, being sycamore, it is very liable to cut very roughly if done lengthwise. This I do with a twenty-two inch trying plane, and having done it to my mind, I take cork rubber, as shown on illustration of tools used by me, No. 67, and rough sand paper, No. 2-1/2, maker's number, and proceed to scour it level--smoothness is not essential.

With compasses 55 (again referring you to tool plate, as I shall often have to do), I find the centre of the wood at both ends, and I make a dot at each, then draw a distinct line down this centre, having placed a straight edge EXACTLY over each dot. And I must insist on this "exactly" wherever exactness that is only a mechanical result can be obtained; in the present instance, mind, any deviation from this base of operations, as I may safely say, will land you in no end of difficulties, as everything must be "square with the fiddle," as we have a habit of saying, though the whole is a matter of curves and lines, there being nothing of squareness about it. Having drawn this decided line, I take my half outline, plate 1, and place it exactly where, by tracing close to the side of it, touching every turn so that there can be no mistake hereafter, nor any "dog leg" nor broken curve, I reverse the veneer (the outline is of veneer) and do exactly the same as before, and you see the whole violin drawn, except that the button at the top of the instrument is in a rough state, and is not finished until the neck be added at the last. Plate 2.

This outline is my own, drawn by me after Stradivari, but not by any means a copy of that master. Dimensions are:--

Length to where button joins the body . . 14-3/8 inches. Width of upper bout . . . . 6-3/4 " " " middle bout . . . . 4-3/8 " " " lower bout . . . . 8-5/16 "

To be certain that my work is correct, I will prove it (for you will have to do so when you begin), ruling a line from one upper point of lower corner to the other; and from one lower point of upper corner to the other, which gives you a square at each end of middle bout.

I take compasses and place the point of one leg on square centre of broad end, and, opening until the point of the other leg touches lower point of upper corner, I describe a curve to opposite point; and I turn the back bottom to top, repeating the same to prove lower corners true. And both stand the test thoroughly.

The next stage, rough as it appears in Plate 3, after cutting, will require great care on your part, or you will spoil your back; please note how it is done by me. I fix it in the double vice, the flat side, where is drawn the outline, facing me as I sit before it on a high stool. With saw 68 in my hands, drawn up taut by the slip of wood at the top tightening the string it controls, I proceed to cut from the top straight down by the button, until I meet the line forming the upper sweep of the back. But you will observe how very careful I am as I prepare to turn the saw from straight to right angle (which is really at left curve at the button). I grease the saw well, turn it at both handles, so that when I again put the saw in motion, the steel lies flat, edges or teeth to the left, the frame of the saw upright.

I hope I have made this sufficiently plain, and that what I have said will enable you to go well round the violin back, guarding the corners, always greasing your saw as you prepare to round them, rather giving them a wide berth than brushing close past, almost touching the line, in a hurry, when snap may go your steel or a corner of the back.

As intimated, you must clear the line by one-sixteenth inch, so that no risk is run by taking too much wood off, cleverly put on again, when matched by an expert, but which could hardly be done by you just yet.

Well, as you see, I have cleared the rough back from the main body of the still rougher oblong wood, and it must now be my business to cut this rough outline to its true form, which is done by looking at the flat side where this pencil outline is, and with a very sharp, flat-ground knife, specially made for violin makers, tool 19. But before this is done, the main body must be reduced at the edges, on the convex or outer side, of course, to about the thickness of three-sixteenths of an inch good, which is a simple matter, if done with one and a quarter inch gouge 43, in this manner.

In the middle of the bench, which will be your general one, and five inches from the edge, cut a one-inch square right through the wood, and fit a long stop therein, the tighter the better, and somewhat rounded off at the inner corner facing you. This will serve to keep one end of back or belly rigid when the other end is provided for, as I do thus:--About fifteen inches from this square top, and to your right, clamp down a piece of hard wood, three inches broad, and a quarter of an inch thick, square with the bench, and on both sides. Then cut a square hole in it, five inches from bench side, to enable you to allow the rough button to lie whilst you operate on one side of the back, then on the other. This, as you must see, enables the wood upon which you are to work, perfect freedom from obstruction of any sort, whilst the gouge cuts roughly all round, as shown in plate 3.

So, leaving the convex side as it is for the present, I resume, as to cutting to the true outline with the knife. You can begin where you like, but I generally clear the right side first. I cut through the pencil line, not entirely obliterating it (which you will not find easy), because, after awhile, I have to efface it altogether with a file, to a perfect, smooth line. These square corners--these curves of top, middle, and lower bouts--all and everything must be well done, and no one thing outside of beauty left for the critical eye to gape at.

Turning the plate to the outer side, I press it flat, between the square let into the bench and the three-inch slip clamped about fifteen inches apart, as spoken of before. This is done so that it may be rigid whilst I take one-inch rasp 47, and proceed to level all round the wood to about five-eighths of an inch and five-thirty-seconds of an inch deep. When I get to the ends of the back I loosen the wood, and use the file more freely at the end of the bench. But this is a matter left entirely to the workman. When this is nicely done, I wet a sponge and damp all I have gone over, surface and edge alike, and let it thoroughly dry, and when it is so, I employ medium cut file 63, half round, seven-eighths of an inch broad, and make the edge of the wood clean, and so even all round, that my first finger or thumb passes over the surface without a suspicion of irregularity suggesting itself. This, mind, must be most carefully done, as otherwise, if you, to make both ends meet, so to speak, take off here a morsel too much, and a little extra there, to repair your fault, thinking to improve your line, you will find it broken, and no longer in uninterrupted movement, as it should be. I would rather see almost anything bad about this noble instrument than a slovenly outline, for it is not only ugly in itself, but leads to other imperfections, and should be most strongly condemned in the modern school; it will most certainly be by me, should a school spring from this book, as is already spoken of as most likely.

The line being right, I next see to the flat edge being strictly of one thickness all round, which I get to my mind by using a cork rubber-tool 67, and about No. 1 sandpaper--maker's number. You can be sure of this correctness by using a sawyer's circular round gauge--and you had best do so.

Now, gentlemen, this brings me to

CHAPTER III.

PURFLING.

There seems a difference of opinion as to where this word originally was used. I fancy in ancient heraldry; but there the word is "purflew" a "bordure of ermines, peans, or furs," whilst the ancients spell it "purfile," a "trimming for women's gowns." Milton says "to purfle--to embroider." So it seems it has ever been used as an ornamental border, no matter what thing it had to grace, for grace it is: and though not essential to the violin in the matter of tone, yet it most certainly is from an artistic point of view; and its absence in an old instrument constitutes the double drawback of being unfinished, and of less, very much less, value.

But it will be asked by some people, who know something of the construction of the instrument, "what has purfling got to do with the making of a violin at this stage?" To which I answer, much, very much indeed from my standpoint, and according to my theory, as I will explain. It will not be denied, I think, that makers have done and now do this ornamental part after the body of the instrument is put together--in fact, the query at the beginning of this paragraph proves it; by whom I do not know, nor advocated by what book. But I ask you, is it not vexatious when all your efforts have been used to work up your surfaces and to round off and finish your edges, you must in a sense undo much of it, temporarily, by using a tool, or tools, to cut the narrow channel for the ornament, and using glue to finally fix it, when some of the superfluous purfling has either to be cut away by a gouge or scraper? And besides, and to me most important, glue, though wiped quickly away with a sponge and hot water, will leave a residue which can never be wholly got out of the pores; and this should not be if you want a brilliant varnish. Of course I mean oil varnish, but am apt to forget this age of cheapness, which flies to easily put on, quick-drying, cheap spirit.

So, as I made it quite clear to you when introducing the subject of these lectures, that it was entirely on my system that I was going to work, so we will now resume, I deeming no apology necessary for occupying your time in denouncing what, should you imitate, would be bad in art.

It is not my intention to go over the various styles of purfling--double, variegated, etc., etc.--but to show you how I prepare and place that which is universal now, the single, composed, as most people know, of two very thin strips of black wood on either side of one white one. But to do this, I must mark, cut and remove the groove in which it has to rest, which requires much explanation.

The outlined back, being quite ready for marking, I clamp down to the bench with two of those marked 11, one at either end, leaving one side of the outlet free. Then I take this specially-made purfling tool, No. 13, with its tracers fixed for marking the two parallel lines about five-thirty-seconds of an inch from the perfect outline of the back, and I grasp the handle in both hands perpendicularly, pressing the revolving wheel against the edge, of course, and keeping the steel markers going carefully and with only slight pressure all round the instrument, stopping without running off at the corners, however. There is, you see, about two inches not marked where the button comes; this must be traced by placing a piece of prepared hard wood, made to touch just the same curve as where the lines would have come had there been no wood there for a button. This must be very carefully placed and traced, as, otherwise, all will not be in correct sweep.

Now, gentlemen, we enter on a difficult stage--nay, two; but then, as I was once asked by a gentleman, "Which part of a violin is the most difficult to make?" I replied, "Every part." But not quite that; still, what I am now going to do is not by any means the least. But you must not lose heart; he who never fights, never conquers; the man who never blundered or made a mistake, never made anything.

Fasten the plate again on the inner part, not the edge, of the bench, so that you can lean over to do what you see I am about to do, and remove cramps as occasion requires. This is a one and one-eighth inch pointed gouge, 54, long ground and very sharp and thin. I grasp it in my right hand, holding and guiding with the left, and gently work to barely the depth of the purfling along one of the two narrow lines, and then the other for a short distance, until I get a somewhat more substantial double line all over the body. But I must warn you respecting the very tender corners. When you are about say an inch from each on both of its turns, work the three-quarter inch gouge, 52, still more guardedly, and barely so deep, and to a very fine point, both curves, ready to receive the two joined pieces of purfling which is to present you with what is called the "Bees' sting." Do all this as well as lies in your power, for upon this channel being well cut will depend much of the success of the whole ornamentation.

Finishing the tracing and cutting the groove, I find tool No. 0, and remove the strip from it, plate 4. And let me here again tell you to be careful, as it is so easy for a chip to flirt airily from either side, or for your tool to probe too deeply and nearly through the wood, putting you--or, more likely, some one else--to trouble and very nice mending ere all is sound. And the corners only look really well and handsome when you find them as on plate 4, because experience tells one the material to go therein can be made to look equally so.

[Illustration: PLATE IV.]

To cut the prepared purfling into lengths (only approximate, exact had better not yet be tried by you), and heat the iron (inside the bending iron) to a good red, but not white heat, is the next thing I do, and, while the tool is getting ready for me, I cut the purfling of the middle bout at one end only, so that I have half of the finely graduated point we see in a corner of a well-wrought violin, the half springing from one of the other bouts forming the complete whole. You must not suppose that the exact length of the ornament is to be measured by you, no, not with unabated practice; you will have to begin with a length always longer than you need, and pare from the points until your lengths fit beautifully before they are fixed with glue--that is, after bending to shape, which I now proceed to do.

Of course, my experience is great, so I manage to get through this very tedious part of the work without breaking the sensitive thread of wood; but I am bound to tell you that you must be prepared for mishaps, as you will be sometimes off your guard and apply force (if ever so mild) to bend what tact, a sort of feeling I may say, and an iron kept hot, can alone achieve. But, if you break, prepare fresh lengths, and again and again; and I warrant your repeated disasters will have something to do with amended touch, and consequently its results.

CHAPTER IV.

BENDING THE PURFLING.

What I have proved is the best way to bend the purfling is this--place the heated iron (plate 5) in the bending socket, and, when all is so that a smart rap of your hand on the metal shows you the warmth is about as you want it, hold the purfling by the left hand, the mitred end to the iron, so that when you bend, by holding, say rasp 47 in the right hand firmly against the point, and letting the heat only make the curve you want, or nearly without pressure, you will, I think, not do bad work.

So I am now ready to fix this ornament in the groove prepared, and have ready thin glue and a table knife to run it there, section by section, as, in cold weather especially, the liquid sets so rapidly.

I select the middle bout of either side (it is not material which) and lay in the glue rapidly, and yet more rapidly the slip for insertion, merely at this stage laying it flat, and going to the lower and upper bouts, joining the corners as mitred as well as I possibly can. Then I press the purfling as deep as it will sink all over, finally wiping all superfluous glue away with sponge and hot water. But I have not done yet, for there may be a weak place or two in my work that glue will strengthen, so I run yet a little thinner all over the insertion, and let it rest until next morning, when it will mostly have sunk somewhere.

When you are at this stage, great headway has been made; but you must now make ready for greater exertions, and prepare to comply with the requirements of the higher branches of this most exacting art, which you will when you model the back as I now begin to do this, which has dried overnight.

But I must pause to make you acquainted with the difference between "outline" and "model" of a violin--not by any means synonymous, as some have supposed and do yet suppose. I ought, perhaps, to have done this before, but will no longer delay.

It always makes me feel very angry when I hear some person, palpably ignorant in the matter, exclaim, "what a fine model" when he or she means "outline." And again, "this is a grand 'copy' of so-and-so," when example of such is meant; how can an example of, say "Mayson" be a "copy" of him? A fine outline will naturally lead you to expect a fine model--that is to say, arching of length and breadth, graceful and perfectly relative as regards proportion, curves, and an unmistakeable oneness of expression, if I may so speak, of every part as a whole, nothing whatever of incongruity or want of symmetry intruding to disturb once and always the gaze of the connoisseur.

But it by no means follows that a grandly carved and completed model has for its counterpart an equally bold yet subtly refined outline; on the contrary, I have seen just the reverse, as I have also seen most wretched modelling wedded to an outline fit to grace the finest instrument extant. But it is not often so, for, as a rule, where a mind is highly gifted, so that elegance breathes in what its body creates, a broken line or curve comes as a great surprise, and one is apt to doubt the same hand fashioned it all.

Be this as it may, call things by their proper names, and in elegant terms where no quaint ones are sacrificed; and if you know better, never let a false epithet pass unchallenged, for I do not see why a refined, but correct, mode of expression should not be as vigorously upheld in this fine art as in speaking of any of its sisters. For surely vulgarity has no right of place in its vocabulary, yet much language that is certainly not elegant, and not of any particular force of expression, finds repose therein; and a really beautiful and great work is neither made more lovely nor more exalted through contact with that which has neither the status of the one nor the other at heart, except that beauty or high estate be ready ministers of a rapacity calculated sooner or later to bring about its own terrible undoing.

So I resume, all being hard and dry, and begin to model the back.

CHAPTER V.

MODELLING THE BACK.

Pressing the plate firmly between the fixed rests on the bench, I take three-quarter inch gouge, tool 22, and proceed to cut a channel entirely round the wood to the depth of about one-twelfth of an inch and about three-quarters of an inch broad from one-sixteenth or rather less, of an inch from extreme edge, and through the purfling, of course. The student will at once see that this is done as a base from which is to spring the arching. There must be no attempt at a finished bend in going over this groove; but there must be the greatest care observed in the cutting of it, as you are using the tool following the outline, consequently, in the manner most liable to encounter disaster in the shape of chips flying from that narrow edging which it is your set business to leave as intact as possible.

After going over the wood in what I call "the guitar line," that is to say, passing by for the present all the corners, I return to them, in my hand gouge 24, three-eighths of an inch, and work them out on the same basis exactly as the main groove. All this being to my mind as shown in fig. 6, I take gouge 43, used before, and in the roughest way possible, and avoiding any depth of cutting, I model the back in its first stage, as shown in fig. 7, obtaining even here a decently developed and somewhat truthful arching all over.

From which I advance to obtain the first smooth stage all over, as in fig. 8, thus--with a square of No. 2-1/2 sandpaper folded in half, so that in size it is about 2-1/2 inches all ways, and this again folded crosswise, giving me a firm point as would be a rasp so formed, I work out the corners, and all about them for, say, an inch, until I get a beginning and an example of groundwork from which to smooth down the whole. Then I take the cork rubber, tool 67, and a piece of sandpaper as last, rather larger than the one just used, so that I can bend it firmly over both sides and as I want, when I change it about to secure a fresh, sharp edge.

I begin by firmly placing the wood, etc., as before, and working the sandpaper (over the cork), firmly pressed in the first stage, against the rough, raised edge, all around the outline, but being most careful not to wear what is left of it away, which must be left intact as far as possible to the end, when it is made to assume that beautiful sort of curled, yet sharp edge so much admired. Then, more towards the upper ridges, over and over, backwards and forwards, having always the careful arching and model of elegance before me, until I arrive at that growing stage of the work as shown in fig. 8, which I proceed to damp well all over with a wet sponge, the surface, as you may see, as I hold it well to the light, being again abominably rough, and not at all now like fig. 8, as the moisture has raised the fibres in all directions.

But before I go farther into this interesting, consequently absorbing process, I must answer some question such as "but why use sandpaper? it is decried by most experts, and utterly ignored by some writers as having no status among the tools used by professional makers of note, and was not believed to have had a place among those of the Ancients."

Then so much the worse for the work of the makers of to-day and for those of yesterday. But who says the ancients did not use it, or crocodile skin, or a cloth made in Venice, and somewhat after our emery cloth? or variously shaped files of different cuttings? At a time when sculpture and very chaste and highly finished woodwork would employ it largely, does any one mean to assert that the violin, not by any means held in the estimation it is to-day, must receive the dignity of small plane and scraper only, and such a useful article treated with contempt because it was what it was? If they do, or any of you do, I should much like to devote an hour privately to any such, when it should be my business to combat such a sentiment, more especially as some writers seem to hint that when sandpaper is used, its scratchy effects can be traced, as I could bring many of my finest efforts to prove the contrary.

My reason for not using small planes for modelling is, that in the first cutting you cannot possibly go over the delicate groove without endangering the surface level--that is to say, if you tear any part in going against the grain (or sometimes with it) and go deeper than you should, would you not at once ruin your even flow of curves as by early arrangement you had set out? your only escape from fiasco being sinking to a lower surface and sacrificing your original conception of true proportion.

Therefore, I stand to the system adopted at the outset of my career, and resume. The wetted surface being thoroughly dry (not apparently so, but really free from any feeling whatever of dampness) I take the next degree towards fineness of sandpaper (or if you like the term "glass-paper" better, by all means adopt it), and I do precisely as formerly, again and again, until six courses have been carefully gone over. Then I go over the same ground six times more, using scrapers 4, 20, 26, 62 alternately, and continually holding up the surfaces to the light as they develop their curves and archings truer and more true, as I scrape here and there with great patience to bring all this about. At this point I suppose you will think the modelling and surface finishing is finally accomplished, and that the interesting passages on thicknesses are about to be written. But it is not so, for the final surface of silk-like smoothness is four or five coats farther from me yet. So I attack with No. 1 sandpaper the surface once more, mostly cross-wise this and all following stages, putting fair pressure and with both hands on the rubber, so that I get sure curves and even surface all over; and then I take No. 0 paper, working well many times round and round by the outline and all over and lengthwise among the curves until I finish this exacting piece of business and fine art, as shown in fig. 9.

And the height of the wood at the middle bout is five-eighths of an inch; at the upper seven-sixteenths of an inch; at the lower, bare half-inch more or less, a fine eye being necessary to discriminate to a hair.

CHAPTER VI.

WORKING OUT THE BACK.

Passing on, I draw your attention to the working out of the back.

I show you, fig. 10, what must be drawn on the back and belly (on the flat, of course) before a chisel touches the wood for excavation. The blocks at either end speak for themselves, they having been fashioned to shape out of Swiss pine, and planed and squared so as to be glued square where you see them marked, later on. And be sure they stand one-and-a-half inches high in the rough, for a reason I will give you later, and about five-eighths of an inch thick, to about the breadth you see on fig. 10.

Before, however, you can do anything in hollowing out the back, you will have to provide yourselves with a bed in which your table must firmly rest while you do so. Therefore, purchase a block of dry beech or birch, about one-and-a-half inches thick, sixteen inches long by eleven inches wide, and lay your finished back in the centre of it, tracing the whole outline, button as well, distinctly thereon; and having done so, cut by the outline inside all round to the depth of about one quarter of an inch, and from this basis proceed to make, as nearly as possible, a counterpart of the model of your back, but reversed, of course. And get all the tool ridges well levelled with rough to fine sandpaper; and, when you lay in your table for cutting, place a strong piece of brown paper for it to rest upon, not only to prevent it in any way scratching the fine surface of your wood obtained at so much trouble, but it enables you to shake off it quickly any residue of coarse dust or small cuttings that will creep under the wood upon which you are working; and so you get on rapidly and cleanly.

You will notice that I have again drawn the guitar line, and at a distance from the outline, so that a sufficiently flat surface is allowed for the ribs to rest firmly upon later. And I cut all round this line just as an indication, merely as a starting point from which to work more deeply all over, until I arrive at a point when the calipers, No. 34, test the thicknesses roughly--which is by the way. For I have first to cut three cross channels, at the upper, middle, and lower nodal points, fig. 11, at such a depth that I caliper good three-sixteenths of an inch at the centre of middle groove, one-eighth of an inch upper and lower, falling away very little to all edges for the present. And I draw a distinct pencil mark through each groove, so that I must be a poor workman indeed if I go through the wood through these bars, as I have known some novices to do, or cannot gauge pretty well all over by their aid before using the calipers.

But you who, when beginning to cut out back or belly, having no sort of experience whatever, must use every care possible, and keep calipers No. 3 (double) going constantly, as, with their aid, you will at once see by the outside half the thickness registered at the inner; then you can pare away with gouges, small and large, and with spoke shaves, Nos. 48 and 53, until you get a fairly sloping and somewhat level surface from bare three-sixteenths of an inch in centre to full three-thirty-seconds of an inch all round by the edges, as shown by calipers.

And thus I come to the first rough thicknesses of the back; and I damp the surface all over as I did the outside, and dry it carefully; for you will understand the necessity for this carefulness, there being some fear of slight warping from the true flatness now the wood is thin all over, if quick, artificial heat be adopted to draw the moisture.

Whilst this natural process is going on, you must take the large calipers and open them at three-sixteenths of an inch. Then hold the plate in the extended left hand by middle bout, inside upwards, calipers and a long lead pencil together in the other; and, beginning at the centre of the plate, draw the calipers carefully from this starting-point all over the rough surface, gauging with your eye for the present any irregularities of said surface; for I want you to mark every part where the points stick, first within a radius of three inches, gradually extending your field of operations, slightly tightening the calipers as you get farther away from your centre, until the edges are finally reached, when you use the double calipers, No. 3, to ascertain the exact thickness at those places.

This being done, and the places marked levelled down, using spoke shaves, flat gouge No. 50, and rough sandpaper 3, take again the large calipers and go over the whole as before, but more carefully; and do this time after time, until the plate is accurately gauged from five-thirty-seconds of an inch centre to the diminution of about a good sixteenth--say one-twelfth of an inch at the edges. My way of working has always been thus, in preference to using what people call "indicating calipers"; and my advice to you is, do likewise, for you not only get over your ground more nimbly, but you can get from your centre more accurately, I maintain, gradation of thicknesses. I give you what I have proved the best thicknesses for my backs, and am pleased to do so to all the world; but if you care to try a hair or two thinner in the centre, adding those hairs to the edges, do so; you will not lose in energy, but you will in timbre, a trifle.

Before finally quitting this hollowing out of the back, gauge for the last time, then use fine sandpaper, and leave no mark of any tool whatever, as by clean work you will be judged.

This question of thicknesses is an important one, but applies more to the belly than the back; and I shall have more to say on this head when I get to that soundboard, merely adding now that the back must never be weak in wood, yet, at the same time, never so strong that a woody tone is the result, inevitable, as the timbre quality is scarcely developed, and without that I never care for it.

It is desirable at this stage that I point out to you how the inner edges of the back are rounded before the ribs are fixed. I use file No. 6, half round, flat side to the wood first, turning to the round side for finish. When at the corners, I employ knife No. 8 in cutting where the file would not do it so well in the early stage, and this file not at all nicely for finish, so I employ a smaller one, No. 9, to these corners, the other all over the rest of the wood, cleanly doing the work so that about one-sixteenth only of the inner edge is rounded off. Then No. 1 sandpaper is used to finish off the work done, and the next stage is glueing on the end blocks, preparatory to fixing the ribs as they get made--of which, later.

So, for the present, I leave the back, and take up the wood you will remember I selected for the front table, or belly, and devote to it a separate section; merely adding that in the course of my work I have so arranged all the thicknesses of the back that it answers to the tone C, which do not forget, as I shall have again to refer to it.

CHAPTER VII.

THE BELLY.

This is the soundboard of the instrument--that which, I suppose, vibrates as fourteen to ten as compared with the back--that is to say, it is recorded that, given equal conditions, such will be the case. It is that which first receives concussion as the bow strikes the strings, which shock travels down the upper surface of the gut from the bridge until the nut at the end of the fingerboard be reached, when it flies under the said string to the bridge again, which communicates the shock to the belly, the belly to the back by soundpost, ribs, neck, scroll, and all about it, to the mass of air in the body of the violin, when comes what we call tone, and rightly do we call it so, if pure vibrations have been brought into play, otherwise noise would be a much safer word to use. Of course, I give you the above in detail: it will appear to you as though the whole of the agitations were simultaneous, such is the amazing rapidity with which all this takes place. And I only give it to show you how incumbent it is upon you to use every care in all you do when engaged in this work, more especially that on the upper table. For no matter how well your back may be gauged, finished, and finally adjusted; or your ribs, how equally balanced one with another or in relative proportions with the whole: if your tell-tale soundboard be defectively wrought, cheeks too much hollowed, or the thicknesses carelessly seen to, there will be beats in your tone, strings irregular, weak notes and strong ones, and a general unsatisfactory result which could easily have been avoided.

But I will get to work on this upper table; and, there being some interesting features to notice as the panorama of its construction passes before your eyes, you will do well to let nothing escape your observation; besides, there is much that is merely a repetition of the working of the back, and which I omit in letterpress.

The said back, you will remember, was in a whole piece--this belly is in two pieces, as I intimated under the heading "selection of wood"; and, as a natural consequence, has to be joined before I can operate upon it as a whole before you. The manner of preparing the two half plates for a joint is this:-- upon this bench I place what is called a shooting board--a board, as you may observe, upon which, near one end, is inserted, right across it from edge to edge, a piece of wood, square with the length, to serve as a stop against which I press what it will be convenient to call one half of the roof of a house, fig. 1, plate 12, lengthwise, which serves to illustrate one half of the belly, thickest edge, of course, on a square with the edge running along by where rests a very choice trying plane, on its side, tool touching this plate, which I hold with my left hand firmly, whilst I shoot the said plane from end to end of the half belly, fig. 2, plate 12. This I repeat on the other half, and then hold them together, flat side towards me, as I raise the two to a strong light, and if no glimmer whatever creeps between the joint, then I call the two plates perfectly united, and ready for the glue to make this absolute. But if they do not appear as I intimate, then you must operate until this very important part of your work be strictly that of a perfect whole; for, remember, as a whole the two parts must remain for as long as the violin holds together, which may be for two hundred years over and above the years that shall be given to you who make it; and this alone should be an incentive to good work.

We now arrive at this joining of the wood for the soundboard, and the glue to be used must be of the best. Not too thin, but sufficiently so to drop freely from the brush used, and clear whilst being tenacious, as felt by pressure between finger and thumb.

As you may observe, I place one half of the wood in the vice of the bench, and on this, the other half (fig. 3, plate 12). With the hot glue to my right hand, I take the loose half of the wood in my left, and hold it against the one fixed in the bench, and upon the two broad centres or outside edges thus exposed, I work rapidly a good layer of the glue, and then, placing them on each other again, I move them very firmly backwards and forwards, and so they are united, remaining in the bench until set.

My dear friends, it is not to be supposed you will do this exceedingly difficult piece of business even moderately well at first; but you will have to do it somehow as a commencement, and I hope I have made all clear to you. Think the thing well over; see your way well ahead; and I am quite sure your success will be commensurate with your endeavour.

From this stage you will have to repeat what was done to the back, until you reach the cutting out of the groove preparatory to insertion of the purfling; and I only stop you here to direct your special attention to one feature of that groove, or, rather, four of the same character, viz., the corners. These, owing to the soft nature of the wood, will be difficult for you to cut out clean, so as to leave the sharp point (so much admired when well done, so much condemned when ill) clear and distinct; and you must use small sharp knife, No. 8, to effect this, not taking the gouge, 52, to the extreme corner when using it near to it, as the pressure would, without doubt, break it off.

Leaving you with this caution, I shall imagine all done as was the work on the back up to cutting the groove after purfling, plate 6, and resume there, for the purpose of warning you that the gouges for this same work on the soft pine, as opposed to the sycamore, must be exceptionally sharp, and you must cut, and very clean, too, or you will tear the wood, and go below your level, as I before cautioned you. More than this I need not say just here, so proceed with the modelling of the belly, on the former lines gone over for the development of the back, with this difference, you must only use coarse sandpaper in the very early stages, and continue the work over more stages by at least three than on the back; for pine takes more readily scratches, and takes them deeper, than sycamore; and more patience in bringing it to a surface like satin, where no trace of scratch from scraper or sandpaper can be detected under delicate varnish.

Then you must continue until the finished plate 9 is reached, only, as I said above, bringing up the surface to a finer state than the back--not to be called waste of time by you on any account, as you will soon understand when you come to find out what a heartless exposer of any frailty is oil varnish.

So at length we come to the hollowing out and to the thicknesses of the belly.

CHAPTER VIII.

THICKNESSES OF THE BELLY.

Cut the three channels across as explained for the back, but in this way:--At the upper nodal point, so that your calipers register bare one-eighth of an inch from one side to the other, centre as well--same at the other node; and at the centre, full--rather over--one-eighth across, all to be for the present only, as a slight correction will be effected as the final stage of the use of the calipers is reached.

Then operate over the whole surface on these lines, taking little or nothing from the extreme edges, because I want you to reserve your strength there in case your pine turns out very active--that is to say, very sensitive to vibration, in which case, mark me, you must keep up your strength of wood, as this extreme activity will not be in harmony with the regulation mass of air in the violin, and the steadiness of tone will suffer in consequence.

And, that you may very clearly understand the reason of this occasional activity, I must tell you that sometimes the wood, in being cut by the saw at the mill, gets a trifle off the quarter on to the slab; and this, coming to the edges, is less able to withstand the strength of the air in its action of 512 beats to the second, say of responsive C; whereas, all being properly and fairly on the quarter, a slight diminution is allowed, and I consider necessary. And I think the above remarks will very fully explain why we so insist on the upper table being never on the slab or near it.

So we will consider the wood roughened out as I directed, and now I must get you to follow me closely whilst I arrange the thicknesses so that I get that tone which I have found the fullest, the most rich in quality, and of the finest carrying power.

I work at the part of the belly which I call the centre, as it is the place where the bridge stands and answers to central node, consequently the middle of the whole construction and of the mass of air: I scrape and level here until I get a fraction, a hair or two less than one-eighth of an inch thick. This I continue along the breast until I arrive at both upper and lower nodal crossings, when I gradually thin off to both ends, the final thickness being at the flat left for the end block when the belly is attached to it, one-thirty-second of an inch less than the centre. And I reduce from the centre of the breast to half-way towards all four edges, top and bottom, about as at the centre, barely, and to the edges, till they register a fraction thinner than at the upper and lower ends.

The above, be it understood, is when finally finished and smoothed down. I now show you with the calipers how accurately the work corresponds with the theory advanced; and on this, my favoured mode of working for the tone so highly spoken of by my numerous admirers, I have no more to say, except to tell you that the wood so finished corresponds in tone to D, and you will still remember that the back was C.

But other thicknesses than these, both of back and belly, are employed; such as thinner in back and thicker in belly; and as used by Joseph Guarnerius del Jesu--the back about such as we have used in this instrument, but the belly a trifle THINNER in the centre than at the edges--they being about one-eighth of an inch. And we have it on record that many of the violins of Stradivari were originally one thickness all over the upper table, barely one-eighth, and about as I use for the lower; would that we could speak with authority on this as on many another point! But many instruments have had wood taken from them by vampires and faddists, and we can not speak with authority as to the vital points of scores of these noble efforts of art, therefore better not lay down laws or adduce supposed facts regarding them, but do our utmost to build up something as noble, and each one of us leave art no worse than he found it, casting reproach and scorn on the utterly indifferent, or the detestable pander or the vampire.

As I have not to recur to the thicknesses again, it may here be a convenient place in which to say a few words on the nodal points in relation thereto.

Many of you may not know what a "node" in music means exactly--some of you may know nothing whatever about it. Simply, it is the fixed point of a sonorous chord, at which it divides itself, when it vibrates by aliquot parts, and produces the harmonic sounds. And do you not see how this struck chord can serve and does serve to illustrate my exposition of the back and belly--more particularly the latter--in their vibrations and their concentration at upper, middle, and lower nodes? To these places they fly, they cling, singly, thin, and of no character; and from these places they again fly, but united in a strong, sonorous tone. How then, think you, will fare those worked out cheeks or attenuated edges, (some of which latter I have seen no thicker than a worn shilling), when worked hard and in a hot room? Gentlemen, they will sound like something between a musette and a Jew's harp, when you are near to the player; they will not be heard at all some yards away! Yet it is such a tone (!) which many hundreds of old violins possess, and after which so many million people run. Please note this is entirely without prejudice. Every person has a perfect right to use his own judgment; and tastes differ.

CHAPTER IX.

THE SOUNDHOLES.

The next operation on the belly is cutting the f or soundholes, and I need hardly say (for it has been so often said, that surely you must all be informed on this point), how the drawing, the placing, and the cutting of this most crucial test of a man's powers as an artist or workman, determines the extent of one or other, or both; for a man may be the one, and show himself a blockhead as to the other. You ask for originality, and you find copy, copy all over the world; yet you may suddenly pounce on a line or two not seen in combination before, most abominably in juxtaposition to their entire opposites in curve as they are in grace as in character. For example or examples, suppose I found, crowning the severe, almost rigid column of the soundhole of Del Jesu, the mobile bend of Stradivari? or, at the turn of the companion lines of Stradivari, the Gothic arch of Del Jesu? with the base of each of a like nature--do you think I should pass such without a severe growl of condemnation? And yet I have seen such; and I scarcely expect to go on to the end without seeing more of such incongruous monstrosities, but I trust not from any one who can give one thought to character as applied to form.

Fig. 13 is a rough example of the soundhole which I shall presently stencil on to the belly just ready for it. As you will notice, the soundhole is cut out of a piece of paper which follows the lines of one of the lower corners. So, upon the corresponding corner of the wood to be cut, I place this that represents the soundhole, exactly; and I dip a small stiff brush into lampblack, not too wet, rather dry than otherwise, and I dab on to the belly through the cut impression of the soundhole--then I reverse the paper, doing exactly the same at the other side of the wood. Of course, I know beforehand that the impressions will be anything but perfect, or clear, or alike; but I have a way of making them so in cutting, and you, many of you, I hope, will soon acquire the same power. The general feeling of active form, as I may say, must guide you; because, to have the stencil plate by your hand as you seek to give vitality to the dead form impressed on the wood, is one thing, but to copy it slavishly, even though it be your own design, is another. In one word, you must always create, no matter what work you are engaged upon, and, in this case, two as original soundholes as lies in your power, and resembling each other as much as you can cut them, but-- cut by an artist.

Proceeding to put you in the way of doing this, I bore a small hole with the little piercer tool 0, and, inserting the fine cutter of fret saw, tool 69, inside the belly, so that I have the upper side to the eye, I press the said fine saw into the slot of the screw, and, with spring pliers 51, I fix it for cutting. Then I hold the belly with the left hand level against the lower part of my breast, and cut out a rough passage round the inner part of the soundhole, never touching the line, though, but leaving that for the knife 8, which follows.

Where I must especially caution you in the use of this fret saw, is at the upper and lower points which face the holes, as they are so liable to snap there, especially at the lower. Still, with care, you will manage to do this neatly and safely, as you see I have done one, and now proceed to work with the knife mentioned.

This knife, as you see, is very much worn, and is very thin and very sharp. And the two latter characteristics it must possess, as you will one and all of you find when you come to use such, for, as I cut from the inside, the steel continually cropping up here and there, in curves and near to corners, I must be prepared at any moment to work up or down, backwards or forwards, with the grain or against it, until I get somewhat of the shape I wish. But not nearly all I want; so I trim the longer lines until they bend gracefully, ready to fall as does the head of a rocket before it bursts, or give a majestic sweep at the base where they terminate in the spread wing. The apertures at the summit and base I round carefully off; the cuts at the centre of the figure, as a break, as finish to what was unfinished without it, and as a guide to determine the position of the bridge.

And you will conclude this finishes the one soundhole; but it does not, for after I have dressed down the work on the outside with No. 0 sandpaper, there is not a clean bit about it--not a curve or sweep or any part true; and when I retouch it all over, and damp it all over after doing that, when it dries, there are still bits I don't like, and patiently trim it and touch it once or twice again, as I have done to many a poem, to be, perhaps, only engraved in water, or ice at the best; typical, not only of its reception by the world, but of its ultimate starvation and ignominious effacement by the coming warmth of an inspiration congenial to all.

This being at length quite to my mind, I cut its companion as true to the lines of the other as possible, fig. 14, when I take in hand the placing of the bass bar on the belly, in the rough, preparatory to toning it down in shape, etc., when the glue has set hard.

CHAPTER X.

THE BASS BAR.

There are different opinions as to not only the function or functions of this bass bar, but as to its length, size in height and breadth, and the placing of it by the soundhole on the G side of the instrument.

As to the former, I think it is pretty well agreed that the bar--only one, please--answers the purpose of a support and vibrator, as opposed to the soundpost, which is of a quite opposite nature, being semi-rigid and a conductor of sound. It is a support where the belly, if too thin, has a tendency to sink; and how often do we notice this, aye, and in (market) valuable old violins too! when bars, out of all proportion to the rest of the work, have to be inserted, so as to keep up a dignity of doubtful reputation! I will try to make this very vital point clear to you. The wood of this belly is very thin and very old, consequently, very sensitive and active, and more responsive than it ought to be to do battle properly with the mass of air inside, fine, solid tone being required. In a measure to check this over activity and give more resistance, this heavy bar replaces the old one; but do you not see that a counter evil results? for the over weight of wood added as a bar is not in sympathy with the rest of the thin table; and this, not being strengthened (as against all the canons of order or of etiquette of the initiated), it still responds as before its old companion was cast aside; and I maintain what is gained in strength is lost in quality, resulting from a jarring of two rival conditions.

As I told you, the tone of the belly was D when I stencilled the soundholes on to it; when I had cut the soundholes, it came to C; and it must be my business to bring it again to D, as I work only on these lines, as, if back and belly be of one tone, or too severed, or the latter, say C and the former D, or near to these, there will be weak and strong tones, beats, and perhaps more than one wolf, and not a result at all satisfactory.

Placing the belly face down in the rest before used when hollowing out, I take a strip of old pine (in fact, cut from this belly itself, when in the rough), eleven inches long, five-sixteenths of an inch wide, one and one-eighth inches deep. I then roughly plane this on the shooting board (the plane on its side as used for shooting the plates of the belly).

In fig. 15 you will see that I place the bar at a slight angle, lengthwise, and close to the soundhole; and you will also observe the small squares of pine glued along the joint, so as to give strength to that joint. And I must tell you to put these squares cross-wise with the grain, as I have seen joints in violins give way, and the bits prove a mockery, as they were placed with the grain, or lengthwise--that is to say, they offered no resistance when the collapse came, but quickly yielded and split as would have done a layer of a turnip! Surely, men must be artists indeed, not to forecast such a likelihood arising as this.

Continuing re Bar, I work away until I get it to fit absolutely to the surface to which I have to glue it; when I slightly thin it in width from the broad end to the narrow of the violin, as I study every possible contingency; and, by not over-weighting the lesser surface for vibration, I give it a freedom otherwise somewhat retarded, even though infinitesimally. And you will wonder why I place it so much nearer the broad end than the narrow--against the laws laid down by the unctuous law-makers of no matter what nationality? Well, it is because I look upon it as a vibrator and as a pendulum; and surely you would never look for the true action of a pendulum, had it a tendency either to one side or another? No, it must work truly and have no bias whatsoever. So, I contend, must this bar, as a pendulum work clean and truly, taking its centre from the cuts in the soundhole, where begins concussion, and the surface of the whole body, wood and air alike. Then why do people act counter to this law, for such it is, and place short bars and long bars, thick and thin, but ignoring this principle for which I so strongly contend as of the greatest consequence? Let them continue to do so, and go on producing tone so satisfactory to them--I advocate an entirely different mode of treatment, as I produce a purity of tone which is a matter of so much comment--and I leave it to your investigation.

The cutting, shaping, and bringing the belly to the note D, by means of this, is part of the work to which you will have to devote great attention: from the shadow thrown by the bar in fig. 15 you will notice that it is shaped somewhat after a gracefully wrought bow, unbent, and at once makes it apparent that it will be a factor for good, as many such have I proved to be.

The reader must not consider the two blemishes on each upper curve of the D as shown on fig. 15, errors in work; they are evidently thumb marks, and dirty ones, through carelessness of photographer.

This brings us at length to the end of the construction of back and belly, both of which we shall leave for the present, whilst we consider the very essential ribs.

CHAPTER XI.

THE RIBS.

The thickness, but more especially the depth of these, is of much consequence in relation to strength and quality of tone. I have found a bare sixteenth of an inch answer very well for thickness, and on the model I have worked on before you, in depth one and a quarter of an inch at lower or broad end, gradually narrowing to one and one-eighth full at the narrow.

Now, take the thickness for granted; but follow me very closely while I describe to you how I arrive at the depth being just what I want and sought for to obtain the note B before the soundpost is inserted, when you blow in the f, C, after it is fixed. Of course, this is making the scientific part of the work, or one of them of no sort of anxiety to you, being already done by me at no little trouble and much thought; but, as I set out as a teacher, if only of moderate calibre, I shall go through with my endeavour to make some good workmen out of my listeners and readers, therefore you are welcome to what is, I think, of importance, never minding what will be said at the outset, that all this fuss is somewhat of nonsense, seeing that it was so easy to copy the depth of a rib, and get to what was wanted and avoid it. But I do not like copying where I can help it; besides, what I shall lay before you has the merit of getting at what you want to a nicety, and of finding out what depth of rib will suit the model in hand, and obtaining the mass of air of which I before spoke.

On a finished back, just like the one which we have before us, I fitted a set of ribs about one inch deep to three-quarter inch taper, and on a similar belly to this, another set of like depth; but I so arranged that those on the back should be one thirty-second more out than usual--that is to say, nearer the edges of the wood--and those on the belly one thirty-second more in, or away from those edges. Then, after filing and scraping for a long time, I, with no little patience withal, contrived so that I fitted one set over the other of the ribs, (as a double box) and got a sort of fiddle body, clumsy of course, but I saw my way to doing just what I had set out to do, and I did it eventually.

Gradually shallowing the ribs by lowering belly or raising back, I got various tones or notes for the air mass, trying E, D, C, B, A, but no resonance such as that of B suited me, so I roughly glued these ribs firmly together, fitted up the whole thing with every accessory such as would allow me to play on the instrument, with the satisfactory result of proving a case beyond question.

So I get to the necessary and somewhat difficult process of making the ribs, etc. But the mould in which they are to be temporarily fixed must be first made by you, and this is the way to go about it.

Get a piece of dry beech--birch or maple of the plain sort will do--18 inches long, 7 inches broad, and 1-1/2 inches deep. Take the half outline of the violin which you have decided to make, and place it flush with the edge of the above block, equal spaces being left at either end. Then very firmly and very accurately draw the half outline on the block for your mould. After you have done this, you must trace an inner line all round the other, one-eighth of an inch from the real outline; and, when you get to the corners, carry this inner line to a broad, open point somewhat beyond the square of the corners, as by this you are enabled to pass your ribs a little over the terminus at said corners, which will most materially assist you to effect a good joint there.

After this is well done, and your under surface quite level with the plane, take the block to a good band sawyer, and get him to saw just through the inner line, and you will have your mould in a measure ready for your ribs. Still, there is something to be done before you can set to work to fashion them, and the first is, square after the fret saw every quarter inch of its work, with steel square, 60, on tool block, your basis being your planed under surface, as most reliable.

Then, about one inch from inner mould, and one inch apart all round, drill holes through the wood with tool 56, or similar; and three larger holes, about seven-eighth inch diameter, one and a quarter inches under the centre of the D or middle bout, the other two some distance under the two corners. The small holes are for the bent steel cramps 2 to hold by when the linings are being fixed to the ribs, etc., and the three larger ones to hold down the centre rib in the same way by means of fitted wood block 33, and for the corner blocks, when they are fitted properly to the shaped ribs. (Cramp 11 is used in these latter cases.)

Having the mould ready, and in good order, prepare your ribs in this manner:-

-selecting what is nearest in figure to the back--good, honest wood--dress down both sides of it, the outer to a more finished surface, of course, and cut them to the dimensions previously stated, viz., one and a quarter inches to one and one-eighth of an inch whole length; but this whole length you will have to determine by measurement of each separate bout--lower, middle, and upper--which, when done to a nicety, mark on respective bouts for all future guidance in exact length.

When finally dressed, cut into lengths, and the ends of the middle rib filed down so as to enable the ends to pass and join upper or lower bout as the case may be, they being filed to fit, put your heating iron, fig. 5, and another iron to match, so that you will have a reserve of heat always on hand, into a bright, if possible smokeless, fire, and from one to the second of the heaters, get a good hot temperature--not scorching, be sure--and place a piece of brown paper over the narrow end of the heated tube. Then hold tool 64 in your right hand, middle rib in the left, and, with one end on the brown paper, the tool on that, very gently, cautiously, and by intuition, as it were, feel your way to a sweet curve of upper corner, using the broad part of the iron for the lower. Of course, although I have not told you, you will have bent the wood face to the mould for this centre, as the reverse for the outer, or larger ones, naturally. This done to your mind--do not be discouraged when I say I hope it may be--for you have hot work before you in more ways than one--get to the sharp corner curves of both the other ribs, face against iron afterwards, inside against it. Mind, as is your true shape to mould, so will your ribs be when it comes to be attached to the back; and there is no patching or trickery allowed here; so do your best. After this, fix the three sections into the mould, and keep them in position by means of cramp 2, and the centre one with block 33, held firmly by cramp 11.

Your corner blocks must be a trifle broader than the ribs, and about as wide as them--also from corner to inner surface, about one and a half inches. Cut and fit these nicely for future glueing, and then prepare and bend your pine for linings. This pine must be about five-sixteenths of an inch broad by about three-thirty-seconds of an inch thick, cut to taper for inner dressing either before or after fixing to ribs. These are not too easily bent, but not nearly so difficult as the ribs; but do not put on too much pressure, or snap is the result.

It will be necessary to see carefully to the gradation of the depth of the ribs from one and a quarter inches to one and one-eighth of an inch, either when they spring from a whole length or from three separate ones. In any case, my advice is to mark the beginning and end of each section from the broad end to the narrow, Nos. 1 to 2, lower; 2 to 3, middle; 3 to 4, upper; so that you cannot well get wrong in bending, from which would spring the first cause of error.

Having your glue somewhat thin but firm, at the point of setting, glue and clamp well your corner blocks (your mould being in the vice) and after that, remove the fitted wood block over the centre rib (it being now fast at both ends by means of the blocks just glued), and accurately fit the two small linings there, removing each end of said lining between block and rib, at either end, and, by first forcing half-inch chisel where the lining will have to go, as a sort of slot. This you must also do at the ends of all the other linings. Now glue the two small ones for centre and carefully fit and force them end by end into slots, finally placing wood block 33 over glued linings, and clamp firmly with cramp 11. The other four are much easier to fit and fix; small cramp 2 being used; but here you must always be sure of a perfect fit all over, or you will find when taken from the mould there will be apertures, Fig. 16.

When dry next day, and before you take from the mould, remove most of the cramps (one or two being left to keep the work fixed) and very neatly cut and clean all the work, as shown in figure of open instrument, and go about it in this manner:--the heavy corner blocks must be reduced with large gouge, and the linings made to fall away from their full thickness at edge of ribs to fine union with said ribs at the extreme of their (the linings) width. After that, clean every atom of superfluous glue away, and finish off with two or even three courses of sandpaper, rough to fine.

Then remove these so far finished ribs, and take the knife 19, being made by you exceedingly keen of edge, and square both edges all over, so accurately that, when they are glued later on to the back and belly, they shall fit and well, being jointed so that no aperture whatever is apparent.

But, you will doubtless murmur, it is all very well to say all this--please show us how to do it all; for, on the face of it, this is no child's play. And you are right to speak out; for it is one of the most difficult points we have to master, and I fully intended to make it quite clear before leaving it.

Hold the rib by left hand firmly to your breast, face side to you. Then take the knife 19, and cut away the superfluous linings and corner block wood, holding the steel absolutely square with the rib, or you will be all abroad. It is this squareness that is the severe test and your great trouble just now. Try on anything and on everything before you try it on a rib you may spoil; but do it on something or other, and finally you will do it and well on these ribs.

But, after cutting, you will have still more to do--lay them flat and keep them so and rigid with left hand whilst you, with rasp 47, fine side, level from one end to the other, not from you across the rib, as the other way is safer for keeping square, and obviates the risk of tearing away part of a lining or slip from a corner block.

You will have dressed the ribs at the outset as instructed; but you will now find them anything but fit to attach to the back; so trim and make them free from any blemish or stain of dirt, and then do your best to fit one side accurately, so that, when glued afterwards, there may be no discrepancies nor goings back.

CHAPTER XII.

FIXING RIBS, ETC.

When you have attached the end blocks to the back, just the width of the ribs and the margin allowed when rib block was made firmly and without cramps, and dressed off next day, fit temporarily the set of ribs just made ready and clamp with the small wooden ones, as shown in fig. 17. You will have made both ends of rib somewhat longer than necessary, and, as they overlap, from inside mark where the top and bottom of linings are flush against blocks at each end. Then detach the rib, and cut away the small bit of lining as just marked. Then fit again, ribs going to end blocks now free, linings flush with end blocks. If not neat in fitting all round, cut the least possible bit away still from linings, until all be perfect. Then square to the exact centre of broad end block, and cut it there; the other end is of no moment, as, so long as the rib is flush with the button, and allows the neck to be inserted neatly, all is right. I hope I have made all this sufficiently plain to you, as the process is of importance. You will gather my meaning best, I think, if you study fig. 18.

In fitting with glue you will now need some assistance. Damp the side of the back, upon which this first set of ribs has to go, with a sponge wrung out of hot water. Then carefully dab on the rib all over the edge to be glued, when your glue is hot, also at each end where it has to join the two end blocks. Then, with loose wood blocks, 66 and 67 to your hand, hold the glued side of the rib over the under part of your glue pot, and then rapidly get all the parts glued well on to the back and end blocks where they are to be. Then fix the block 67 at the narrow end, and get your assistant to clamp it with tool 11-- and the broad end with block 66, going to the small wood cramps for the rest of the fixing round the half of the instrument. See fig. 17.

This does not seem to have a ring of difficulty about it: but it is difficult-- hedged around by it, but not, even to a nervous amateur or novice, insurmountable. Do all the work clean as lies in your power; have everything ready to your hand; act firmly as you can, and rapidly, whenever you have glueing in hand, and the result, be sure, will be in accordance. The second set of ribs is treated in every respect as the foregoing.

Every particle of superfluous glue must now be removed, in and out, and from the inside any ridges round by the ribs, and all smooth, level, and open to inspection now, as in the course of years it is all sure to be; for no instrument is so liable to damage as the fiddle, and you never know into what studio your beloved one may go, or by whom it will be criticised. And apart from this latter consideration, pride in your own work and love of truth ought, and I hope will, actuate to noble effort; but mind, do not overrate what is done, in your pride of heart, for those into whose hands it will come later will assuredly not do so.

When you have cut out the slot at the narrow end into which, later, the neck has to be glued, and made the end blocks level for the belly to rest perfectly, you have practically finished the body of the violin. But I must first tell you how to set about cutting the groove at the end of the instrument, into which the neck has to be inserted. You will note (fig. 19) outline of scroll and form of pattern by which you will be guided in cutting groove for neck insertion. This latter is one and nine-sixteenths of an inch deep--one and seven-sixteenths of an inch broad, tapering to bare one inch at junction with the button. Place it accurately with the instrument, mark with sharp tool, then cut out as you see it is done by me (plate 18).

After this, with brace 29, inserting brace bit 37 at position 28, make a clean cut hole in centre of broad end of violin for the end pin later; and when I have inserted the label, the putting on of the belly is my next work.

As many of you doubtless know, I am credited with a fad as regards this label business. But I do not see why I should be, seeing that so many frauds have been perpetrated in relation to old instruments, aye, and to new ones--my own not excepted. If I write with my own hand all that is written on all labels appearing in my violins, etc., and choose to give each one a name, and register every one in a book specially prepared for reference in the long future, a consecutive number being noted in each in private mark, where is the fad? Will it not be utterly impossible under this system to pass off anything spurious? I think so: and am sure the whole world would to-day be only too glad if the old masters had been silly (?) enough to have fads of a similar nature.

CHAPTER XIII.

FIXING THE BELLY.

The label being fixed with thin glue, and all being in order, see that your cramps, both of iron and wood, and accessories, are all well to your hand, for this is a process where quick action is imperative. Your glue must be hot, and about the same consistency as when the ribs were fixed; and broad pieces of stiff cork must be procured, because the pressure of cramp 11 on back and belly at both ends will necessitate these safeguards.

In the first place, temporarily fix the belly, making as accurate a piece of work of it as you can, exact in overlapping as is the back, if possible. Then get your assistant to clamp it here and there with the wooden cramps, as fig. 17. Afterwards, pierce each end of belly with a bit about three-thirty-seconds of an inch, three-eighths of an inch deep through the table into each end block. Then remove cramps, and, into the holes in said table, fix a small pine peg, about as will just drive home when all is fixed and glued.

Now, wet with a hot sponge all the belly where junction with the ribs has to take place, and then dab a nice layer of your hot glue all round the ribs and end blocks, going over it a second time rapidly, and finally holding every part glued for a second over the hot water under your glue pot. It is urgent that the pegs are then inserted into the holes mentioned above, and that you at once force them home with the smart blow of a hammer, when your assistant begins to clamp as you direct; for there may be parts where a little humoring of either rib or belly will tax your ingenuity, so as to make a neat fit. Then, when all are on fairly well, clamp the ends with the iron cramps, having the blocks of cork to intercept, as spoken of above. (See fig. 20).

When the glue is dry and hard, on the following day you must clean all of it away that is showing and superfluous, and use gouges, 52, 54, 22, chisel 21, scrapers 26, 62. Any cutting of the wood is objectionable; but if there must be a trifle taken away from some part of the ribs to make a bad fit nearer a good one, then be certain to make all smooth with scraper and sandpaper, over and over again, or your work will be uneven at the finish; and your varnish is a terrible shower-up of bad work, my masters.

Following the above is the careful rounding of the edges of under and upper tables with files and glass-paper, as previously shown on the inner edges of the back and belly. Not too broad must this be done, or the somewhat sharp edge which you seek (or should seek) to bring neatly along the centre of the edge, as it were, of a small wave, doubtful whether to curl over on to the body of the violin or not, will lose much in form, and the grace intended be negative, if not utterly lost when under the eye of the connoisseur.

When this is all done, and the corners left beautifully square, save that the sharpness of the terminals are just a little rounded off (not the two points-- these must not be touched) wet all you have gone over with a sponge, and clean when dry with No. 0 sandpaper, until you are sure your work will do you credit under the varnish, when you arrive at that stage. Before that, however, we have to consider the cutting of the scroll.

CHAPTER XIV.

THE SCROLL.

On plate 19 you will find the outline of a scroll I use generally. I will employ the original from which this was taken now, and mark on a piece of old sycamore the exact representation of it.

The thickness of the wood must be one and eleven-sixteenths of an inch, ten inches in length--and broad enough to allow the outline to be properly cut for further operation. After I get this cut exactly by a band saw, I place the outline on the wood cut for the scroll, and with a sharp-pointed, hard pencil, prick the holes where the volute has to come on to the sides, both of them. After that, on the face of the wood--that is to say, the front, as though looking at the fingerboard, I mark at four-and-a-quarter inches from end of the head, which is to be the end of peg-box, and three inches from that, the narrow end of said box that is to be cut. Then I take centre of narrow end and mark off seven-sixteenths of an inch--width of said end, five-eighths of an inch for broad end. Then at five and five-eighths of an inch from broad end of peg-box, I take centre of extreme end of wood, here to be one and three-eighths of an inch when ready for the fingerboard afterwards, and I divide it, making a distinctive mark as to breadth and centre. Then, allowing full three-sixteenths of an inch for cheeks of peg-box, I draw two lines, one on either side of centre line, from end of wood to head, so that I just shall catch outer side of each cheek of peg-box that is to be, and which, running on to where crosses the nose of the scroll, gives a width there of bare nine-sixteenths of an inch. Afterwards I mark the three-sixteenths for cheeks of peg-box.

This is all I can mark at present, until I cut with the saw and with the chisels, as shown (figs. 21 and 22), I can now trace lines ready for manipulation of the volutes and the fluting. That of the volutes is my first business. The lines denoting the ascending spirals, and the pencil dots not yet touched, are my guides, and, with small hand saw, No. 30, I cut very carefully, by a dot at a time just low enough to touch the spiral line at its junction, cutting the bit away sideways, of course, just by the said line, and then a small piece more, until I arrive at the end of where the spiral ceases, at its base; but now that the volute is developing, I am enabled to complete the line, which brings the whole to its actual junction with the mainspring of conception. This, in a very great state of roughness, I show at an angle (fig. 23), and I reverse the sides, cutting the other in the same manner. It is necessary to have the wood firmly cramped to the bench on all occasions.

I now select gouges 57, 24, 22, 43, 39, 50, and I carefully trim both spirals, gauging the front and rear levels as I proceed by one-eighth of an inch at a time, until I can find no fault, all being square to the eye (for by nothing else can you prove your work here) when I prepare to cut the trench which was only wanted to soften off this essential to beauty.

Here I use all the gouges marked above; and in doing so I have to be most careful not to FORCE any one part; for such is the brittle nature of the wood (sycamore) that the delicate edges, as the slender spiral ascends under your, perhaps, too eager hand, may not be able to bear the strain put upon them, and a breach stares you in the face, past remedy, save by an accomplished master of his art.

The next step is to soften the work done, and to smooth down with rough to fine glass-paper, wetting every part after each course. Then I cut off all the sharp outer edges, from the terminal of the back part of the whole to the top of each volute, this cutting to be a good one-sixteenth of an inch broad, neatly filing and sandpapering the same when done. The outer edge of the peg-box is done in like manner.

Fixing the wood now, face downwards on the bench, I begin the cutting of the fluting at the upper part, using gouges 57, 24, 22, just in the order in which I write them, obviously the terminal part being that which needs most attention and care. Reversing the wood, I cut down by the nose of the head to the broad grooves which soon appear, terminating just over the narrow end of peg-box. All should be done neatly,--in a masterly manner were better--I file and sandpaper over and over again until I get to my mind what now appears in plates 24 and 25, and you will see the neck end is finished, ready for insertion in the mortice, which is done later when the fingerboard is added.

CHAPTER XV.

FIXING NECK, FINGERBOARD, ETC.

As this neck and mortice business is very difficult of manipulation, I will direct you how to cut the end of neck so that a perfect fit may be obtained in the body of violin where was cut the mortice previously, fig. 19, into which said neck has to be inserted. To the exact outline of this I now cut the neck end, one and three-eighths of an inch broad at top, one and three-sixteenths of an inch at bottom, and one and nine-sixteenths of an inch deep. I cut on an angle, so as to get the elevation required for correct height of bridge. And then, all being square, I slope to the end which is ultimately to be joined to the button. You will gather all this from plates of scroll.

To obtain the peg holes, I mark at certain distances a guiding point, through which, at one side E and A, and on the other G and D, I bore preliminary holes with hand bit No. 12 (on tool plate), square, absolutely, through to the other cheek of peg-box. After all are done, in brace bit 29, position 28, I place taper bit 59, and cut, E, A, D, G, finishing approximately for pegs with tool 15.

Then, before I fix the neck into the violin, I attach the fingerboard and nut--the latter in rough ebony, as I always work this neater with some wood over and above what I want. This fingerboard must be perfect in fit, put on with very hot, thin glue, and well cramped with three No. 11 cramps, having wood guard 31 over fingerboard for protection. When set and hard next day, I prepare the end incision for the neck to enter, and proper elevation of the ebony, so that the correct angle for a bridge of fair average height may be obtained. I give you what is a fair average height--one and three-eighths of an inch; but there is no absolute rule as to this. What is here given is that which will suit the instrument just made, as I know by many constructed on similar lines. This height is got when the bridge is held down by the strings, and the measurement is from belly to middle of the arch of the bridge.

Your fingerboard must be at such an angle when the neck is fixed, that the end of it near bridge must measure exactly thirteen-sixteenths of an inch from belly to top of ebony; by this means your bridge, as described, will be just a nice height for clean fingering of the strings.

This brings me to fixing the neck, and I do it thus:--In the first place, I have to remember that the length from nut on the fingerboard, inner side, to the bridge, must be, when all is finished, thirteen inches exactly, and the angle as above. So I have to be very careful that too much is not taken out of the slot I have to finish, either in width or inner recess, as that, one or the other, would necessitate lowering the neck end, which is not what I want to do. First the knife, then the files (coarse ones), and, little by little, I get nearer and nearer to a fit, when I try angle and the straightness of the whole with the fiddle, using compasses to measure from inner point of purfling, upper corner, to corner of fingerboard on corresponding side, with their exact counterparts on the other; and testing height of fingerboard from belly. This is very weary work, and must be quite correctly done, or--well you will either hear of it again in words, or see your failure in the sweet smile which is more detestable than the severest frown.

But all is at length right; the neck is forced home, and I mark round the button, on to the superfluous wood of neck, its curve, so that I may not cut beyond when I thin the neck to its proper and final shape and thickness.

Many of you will, doubtless, be players of the fiddle, and to such, good, bad or indifferent, I need hardly say how much the disposition and general character of the neck of your instrument influences your performance on it. It is obviously quite impossible to lay down any rule or law, as to depth, width, or the curve at the end terminating at the button, for some will have this latter thin and abrupt, others less so, whilst a few insist on its being thick.

If people only knew how much the strength of the neck has to do with the tone of the instrument, they would leave to the maker or expert to determine what was best for it, either in the original making of the violin or in placing a new neck in an old one. But it is convenience--what we like and what we will have; so, in consequence, suffers the tone of the instrument.

You have a violin thick in wood: if I find on it a neck also heavy in material, to a certainty I have to register thin, woody tone; whereas, given a thinner neck there would be more vibration in it, and an undoubted impetus would be given to the somewhat inert body of the violin--its heavy timber being too much for the mass of air, which acts its part in that it moves in response to compulsion, but fails, in producing so feeble an agitation of the whole wood.

But, on the other hand, I find a thin neck attached to a thin body, and I also find a whole pack of wolves, hollow, rasping tone, and difficult of production--in fact, a wretched fiddle.

Then, as to width of fingerboard--a narrow one is often clung to as "so nice and handy," etc., but it is forgotten that the strings in consequence have to be brought closer together than clean fingering requires; and, moreover, the E string must, of necessity, be brought too near the edge of the ebony for firm stopping; so I have no sympathy whatever with a narrow or too thin fingerboard and neck.

But I have to work away at the rough neck after having traced the outline of the button upon the under end of it--not the actual shape of this necessity, but such as will serve as a guide to one of more grace. Added to that, I roughly mark the shape and thickness of the wood up to which I have to cut away, to insure nice handling. To this line I cut with bow saw 68; and I then use all the knives I have, and many files--rasps in the early stages--until I get to the shape I want, after which I wet with a sponge, renewing the work when dry with finer files and glass-paper, No. 1-1/2, making a second stage, then wet again, to two more stages, when all should be very clean and nice. Of course, I round the fingerboard's edges somewhat, and clean on each occasion of wetting. When finished, the neck should measure round thick end (one and a half inches from extreme end of wood), three and a half inches; and round thin end (one inch from peg-box) three inches. This finishes the neck, which is now ready for insertion in the violin.

I have, above, treated of this: I now do it actually. I have wood guard 31 ready for protection of fingerboard, and 32, for the back, and one of No. 11 cramps. I dab the neck and the cutting with hot strong glue, and gently work them together, until the glue oozes out at all points, when I put on the wood guards and clamp hard. Then I wash the superfluous glue away with a sponge wrung out of hot water, after I have tested whether I have got in the neck straight and at its correct angle. (See fig. 27.)

[Illustration: PLATE XXVII.]

But there is the neat finishing off of the neck and button, which I attend to carefully, when all is set hard on the following day, paying much heed to grace and character here, as it is a part of the fiddle which cries out at once if slovenly, or ungainly, or the least bit out of line or centre.

And I fashion the nut over which the tail-piece gut has to stretch, and cut the bed into which it is glued. Then I very carefully wash the violin all over with a clean sponge wrung out of warm water, giving it plenty of time to dry before I finally clean every part thoroughly with No. 0 glass-paper--and the violin is finished in the white.

CHAPTER XVI.

OF VARNISH AND VARNISHING.

To write an exhaustive essay on this most absorbing subject before us, to go into any manner of detail at all in the present work, is not my intention. It is far too wide, too subtle, and, in my opinion, is an art of itself, requiring not only great space in which to voice its merits, its component parts, and the thousand and one compounds in which those parts assimilate, but the calm of the study rather than the bustle of the workshop, given out deliberately by him whose conclusions are based on the sound issues arising from momentous research, careful analysis of former old examples, and an utter abhorrence of prejudice, for or against this or that compound or colour--prejudice, mind, actuating choice.

But in continuation, though somewhat in parenthesis, a choice based on determined observation of a matter is quite another thing; and I tell you at once my experience as between spirit and oil varnish condemns the former, whilst it very strongly advocates the latter; and when one considers that it is in the nature of oil to assimilate with wood, and to throw up its beauties, and whilst a mellowness clings to the very name, the reverse on all points being the case with spirit, the surprise is that varnish other than of oil should be tolerated.

Besides, see the difference in wear. Use a violin coated with spirit, and if the friction from its employment be severe, you have cracks, pieces chipping here and there, the instrument getting barer and barer daily, so that in time little of it, the varnish, is left. But it is not so with oil; the wear is wear, not in chips, but in gradual diminishing of its substance, always a something being left; added to which a beauty springs from such, in that softer gradations of colour radiate and form a greater depth, from the fact of such colour or colours being more readily absorbed.

Again, in their relations to Tone, I place the oil varnishes first; and I think the point is pretty generally conceded, for what is on the face power, which some attribute to the brittle, assertive nature of the gums hardened by alcohol, is not in reality such, but often aggressive noise, losing itself the more you retreat from it, leaving real tone little to say for itself.

But coat the violin with oil; you certainly cannot complain of loud, rasping responses to the call of the bow, whilst you can make some assertion as to quality. And, remember, as the soft nature of the oil assumes a harder tendency day by day, so will increase the sonority of the tones, whilst retaining the beauty of character with which they began. Therefore, I shall draw your attention to the use of oil varnish, utterly discarding that of spirit.

But to what oil varnish is not my present purpose; why should I seek to close the door on research and on experiment? It is for you, students, to take home, each one of you, the lesson of the mighty failure of thousands gone before you, in inability to bring to a finish that upon which they have spent so many anxious hours, and do something different and better. It is my intention to teach you, step by step, how to lay on what you prepare for the brush: but not to say "get this or that oil," or "this or that colour," except in the abstract--red, orange, amber, yellow, etc., etc., being names only.

I say this at once so that there may be no mistake--so that none can say I use this or that: my own varnish and colouring are my own solely, and I reserve the secret for the benefit of my family, should it prove of value after my career be ended.

Fashion a piece of wood so that it fits easily into the hole at the end of the violin in which, later, the end pin is inserted. It must have a rough sort of handle, because by it you will hold the instrument when you have occasion otherwise than by the neck; for you must on no account touch the wood before you varnish, nor afterwards, with your hands, nor must you allow others to do so, when, in your pardonable pride of heart, you show your creation to your friends.

With a clean sponge, wrung out of tepid water, and a camel-hair brush for parts where the sponge will not be of service, go all over your violin, but do not wet it heavily--far from it; and when quite dry, on the slightly roughened surface thus left, place a yellow or amber coating of turpentine, thoroughly mixing with it a little of the oil varnish selected by you along with your colouring matter as you arrange, yellow or amber. To do this well, and for future use, you must have half to one inch flat camel-hair and fine hog-hair brushes. A round hog-hair brush, medium size, is good for this initial coating (some call it sizing; but I think this is misleading--"size" being generally understood to bear reference to glue, and we want none of that under varnish.)

This should be dry in about two or three days, when you may lay on a second course, less turpentine and rather more varnish; also less yellow and a very little red. This will take somewhat longer to dry, and please observe that the more varnish (if it be oil and gum, pure and simple) so much longer it will be in drying; and, as you advance to the final stage, you will gradually discard the turpentine altogether, as you will the yellow, colouring at last with red only.

As you advance step by step, and before you venture on another layer, with the tip of your finger test the varnish, and if there be the least tackiness, wait a day or two until all be dry. And as a roughness is bound to show itself as stage after stage is passed, it is well to smooth down each course when dry with fine No. 0 glass-paper upon which is first spread a drop of pure Lucca oil, which, of course, must be lightly applied to the body of varnish, and the whole carefully wiped with clean linen or silk handkerchief afterwards.

Now, after the first two coats, you must use about a three-quarter inch fine hog-hair brush (not many hairs in, mind) and for the later coats one with camel hair. Sit on a low chair, have the light to your right hand, the varnish before you handy, not too high. The violin is held by neck, left hand of course; the stick at the broad end through the hole where comes later the end pin (see above) rests on your right leg as you sit. Get a fair dip of varnish in your brush, but NEVER flood it; and beginning carefully under the fingerboard, first one side, then the other, working the top sides of the instrument also alternately, until the soundholes be reached, when inside these cuts must be neatly coloured, after which you just tip your brush with the varnish, neatly continuing where you leave off, so that none can see a break in your progress. This advice applies until ribs and scroll be all done after the belly and the back. I have ever found the upper table the most exacting and difficult; but, once again, never flood your brush, and you will varnish sooner or later. But never hurry: and this advice applies to every thing you do in the construction of the violin. Patience of no ordinary character you must exercise; if you have it not it will come to you, but through experience alone, through failures, through catastrophes innumerable. But what then? These things that have mastered you stand mastered in turn in the excellent result of to-day, so let yesterday go to the wall.

Now that we can consider the operation of varnishing at an end, the instrument is hung on a wire, free to the warm dry air of a room or to a passage where a current of it is circulating. When hard (and there is no actual time to gauge this by) prepare to finish off and rub down the whole; and care must be observed that no scratch appears, for a surface looks bad, very bad, with anything of this sort to mar its beauty.

The first essential in this process is pure Lucca oil, which does not clagg; and the next, specially prepared pumice stone powder, which must be as fine as flour; and should there be any doubt about its being absolutely free from specks of grit, filter it through fine muslin or silk, and only use that which passes through, in water.

Then take some brown paper and make a pad, rubbing on oil and a sprinkling of the pumice stone powder, when you can go over portions of the back, very lightly feeling your way to see whether all works smoothly and no scratch in the operation. If this be so, continue on these lines, sparingly adding more powder, but freely using the oil. You can, to smooth off, use saturated rag (oiled) and after that, a dry pad of very fine muslin or silk.

The belly is tedious, more so than the back, and the ribs still more so. Contrivances to get into corners and curves of the latter, you will have to resort to, such as small pieces of paper, and pumice stone and oil, and oiled fine glass-paper, and finely rubbed pieces of curved wood, with which you can operate to smooth near edges of ribs, etc.

All can be done well, all must be done well; for, remember, there is to be no French rubbish (polish, I mean), on the top of this oil varnish, but your hand must finally bring up its lustre, as I can show you mine has so frequently brought to a rich glow that preparation made and used by me, on my own work only.

CHAPTER XVII.

FITTING UP FOR USE.

This last of many complicated and difficult stages must be entered upon with a will, and great attention paid to all details. The fittings used must be of the best, and the strings rough Roman, and must be tested to see if they vibrate truly. This is done by twanging, so that two distinct outlines are shown; if any dimness appear, or the lines wobble, as I may say, try again, for such are false. Not always, though; for I have known this rule (for it is a rule) falsified, and a good string appear untrue by test, and vice versa.

Take the Rimer, 15, and work out the peg-holes nicely; then fit ebony or rosewood pegs as you fancy, cutting off the superfluous pieces which obtrude on the off-side of peg-box. Apply a little soap and chalk to ensure close working when tuning.

Then on the nut, cut the narrow channels over which the strings have to pass to the fingerboard. A nice discrimination must be observed here as to the width from E to A to D to G. There can be no rule laid down, because some players will have them nearer together than others, and must, if for double stopping, they having narrow fingers; and on the contrary, wider apart, if for broader ended fingers. What I find a nice medium is seven-thirty-seconds of an inch from the bottom of one slot to another. Take the compass and divide to seven-thirty-seconds of an inch and press one point at G, D, A, E, allowing a fair margin at both sides of the ebony, not above, say one-eighth of an inch good. Then use either of the rat tail files, 27, and carefully file to depths required, which must be so as to allow a playing card to slip comfortably under the E string when taut, a little more space for the other three being necessary, especially the G. Rub a black lead pencil through the cuts, and work them very smooth with a thin, round piece of steel, which makes all the strings much easier to slide afterwards and minimises breakage.

The nut must then be filed and sandpapered nicely down to the cuts, so as to leave only a shallow passage, as one too deep retards free action of the string and somewhat of vibration, besides making the fingering less satisfactory. The ends or sides must be made beautifully even with the neck and rounded and papered off so that not an atom of friction worries the player, who has often worry enough in all conscience in the work of correct manipulation before him, without the hindrance of bad work on his instrument.

Then we come to the bridge--with two feet, not more my friends; the dear old fiddle has managed these three or four hundred years to crawl along very respectably as a biped: I shall have nothing whatever to do with turning him into a quadruped, be assured.

The importance of the quality and of the correct height, thickness, etc., etc., of this most essential adjunct, cannot be too seriously impressed upon all who seek to get from the violin they are fitting up the strongest and the best quality of tone possible; and, unless the clever amateur be sufficiently so to do it as it should be and can be done by an expert, my advice to him is, do not attempt it as a work of finality--try to do it properly and persevere, and I will help you. But do not show me with pride work to which attaches nothing but condemnation; too thick at top and bottom--feet clumsy to a degree--too high or too low--badly arranged for clean bowing on separate strings, and too deep or too shallow in the cuts for them. What does it matter to me if only a few or but one of these faults be apparent? the bridge is not perfect, and perfect it must be made, so I proceed to the consideration of the work to be done to make it so.

Select a fine, strong, light bridge by either Aubert or Panpi--the former by preference. In using the names of these deservedly popular makers, I mean, of course, either Aubert or Panpi, and the bridges wrought in their workshops, not the nasty imitations we are compelled to see sometimes, but which, rather than use, we would go a day's journey to avoid.

Pare the feet down to about one thirty-second of an inch (this when fitted finally) and proceed to make as accurate a union of these feet with the belly as you can, as it is most important that such should be the case. Then measure the height of this bridge, from belly to its top at centre, as one and five-sixteenths of an inch, nicely curving it so that ease of bowing is obtained, as spoken of before. This curvature should be unequal in height--or, rather, to express it better, the height on the G side should be so that, at the broad end of the fingerboard, the space between the ebony and the string will be a quarter of an inch, reducing as we get to the E, which registers about one-sixteenth of an inch less, or three-sixteenths of an inch. This is a guide, and a good mean to work on, but not a rule, as some people cannot play except the strings are near to the board, others just the reverse.

As to the distance between the strings, where they pass over the bridge, this is also a point somewhat of controversy, and applies, as do my remarks in reference to the fingerboard nut--there is no rule; but a very useful mean distance is seven-sixteenths of an inch. When you have got the angle correct, mark with the compasses where the incisions are to be made with tool 27 round, rat tail file, and work the cuts accordingly, about as deep as the file where it tapers one-third from its point.

Then reduce the bridge in thickness from its feet upwards--very sparingly at these feet, but tapering to pretty thin at the top, say a bare sixteenth of an inch. The reduction must be made by rubbing on sandpaper, and a clean, straight tapering effected, as a bridge, where you can discern a round-backed slope, is bad--looks so and is. When fitted and completed, the bridge must be as near perpendicular as possible; if there be any inclination, it must tend to the tailpiece, and very slightly, thus checking the certain tendency of the strings to pull it forward, which must be always closely watched, as if it fall on the belly of the violin, it is most liable to break--not only so, but to crack that same soundboard. The outer edges may be either filed to an angle of one-sixteenth of an inch bare, or neatly rounded.

The soundpost must engage your closest attention, and must be of old Swiss pine. There is, again, no rule as to thickness--some violins do best with a thick, others with medium to thin post. I only tell you for guidance, a medium to thin is mostly used by me. It must be evenly rounded, and both ends filed so that the angles of back and belly may fit exactly when it is placed inside. To get the exact length is not an easy matter; but you will find this hint useful: with a thin piece of wood gauge the depth through the upper hole of the soundhole from the back to the outer surface of the belly, and your post will have to be a trifle longer than this, minus the thickness of the belly. Then take a soundpost setter and fix the pointed end into the wood, sloping sides towards you, of course, and do your best to place this most exacting, but most necessary adjunct, just behind the centre of the foot of the bridge on the E side--the distance of about a good sixteenth of an inch behind the side next to the tail piece. When fitted, it must be neither slack nor tight, but between the two.

Of course, this operation will be, to the novice, a horrible job: he will fume and he will perspire, and, I fear, he will use strong language--none of which will help him, but on the contrary, will retard progress. The thing has to be done, and done well; and it would be much better if the amateur cannot do it ultimately, to pay an expert for timely instruction.

Then fit the end pin, but, before doing so, look through the hole in which it has to go and ascertain if the post inside be straight--which is very necessary to the good ordering of pure tone. Regulate with the broad end of the setter, and draw or push through the soundhole on either side, as may be necessary.

And when you have nicely gauged and secured by single knobs the tail-gut to the tailpiece, the instrument is finished excepting the neck, the polishing of which we will now consider.

With constant handling you will find this neck dirty and greasy. Wash it well with a sponge, and when dry, colour with a yellow water or spirit wash. Do not sandpaper at all yet; but make a nice orange-coloured spirit varnish, and place neatly over the yellow three or four coats. When thoroughly hard, clean it down with No. 0 sandpaper soaked in Lucca oil, smooth, and ready for the hand.

CHAPTER XVIII.

CONCLUSION.

Then, my friends, reward your many anxious moments of thought and work--string your fiddle, for, be assured, you will be rewarded, be your instrument somewhat crude in tone; and he is of a miserably cold, prosaic temperament indeed, who does not warm up at this juncture--this climax, this crisis. It may be the tone is good, very good; with what pride it is shown and tried; should it be mediocre, or even poor, a certain amount of pride is excusable, and faults are condoned.

Should there be faults that a touch of the soundpost may minimise, gently touch it, moving it hither and thither, until it meets with a desired response. Or your strings may be too thick or too thin; all may be of no avail, however, so work the fiddle for six months, and note if it shows signs of improvement; if not, look well to your construction next time, and build for posterity on early failures, on disappointments after long study and careful manipulation, or resolve to be master, after hearing your praiseworthy devotion rewarded by the empty sneers of those who, maybe, care nothing whatever whether you do ill or well, but only that they have the chance of showing their superior wisdom and making stagnant that which, given warm encouragement, would have flowed on until the future would proudly record the noble work of real genius.

THE END.